THE FJH
CLASSIC MUSIC
DICTIONARY

Edwin McLean

Editorial assistance: Karyl Louwenaar
Italian pronunciations: Luis M. Quesada
French pronunciations: Camille Henderson
German pronunciations: Wiltrud Bering Georges
Design: Terpstra Design
Production: Ika Simpson

THE
F·J·H
MUSIC
COMPANY
I N C

Abbreviations used in this dictionary

abbr.	abbreviated	It.	Italian
c.	century	F.	French
ca.	circa (approximate)	G.	German
cap.	capitalized	Sp.	Spanish
e.g.	for example	L.	Latin
esp.	especially	Gr.	Greek
i.e.	that is	Brit.	British
pl.	plural	Eng.	English
v.	verb	Russ.	Russian

Many individual terms in the dictionary are cross-referenced to larger essay terms, which are displayed in all capital letters. For instance, if you were to look up "cambiata," you would be referred to NONHARMONIC TONES – where all of the nonharmonic tones are explained within a proper context. For convenience the essay terms are listed below:

bowing
brass instruments
electronic music
Gregorian chant
harmonics
history of western music
interval
inversion
key signature
Mass
meter
minor scales
motion
nonharmonic tones
notes
(incl. table of note and rest values)

opera
orchestra
(incl. names of orch. instruments)
organ pipes
pedal
percussion instuments
pitch names
serial music
seventh chord
sixth chord
sonata form
symphony
violin family
woodwind instruments

These terms were chosen not necessarily by their importance, but by the fact that there are usually a large number of terms associated with them. It is hoped that this contextual approach will help the reader achieve a more complete understanding of a particular subject.

Arranged in order from slow to fast.

Adagissimo	extremely slow
Lentissimo	slower than Lento
Lento	slow
Adagio	"at ease," slow
Adagietto	faster than Adagio (and lighter)
Largo	slow (broad)
Larghetto	faster than Largo
Andantino	usually slower than Andante (sometimes faster)
Andante	walking tempo
Moderato	moderate
Allegretto	not as fast as Allegro
Allegro	fast, "cheerful"
Vivace	lively
Vivo	vigorous
Presto	quick, fast; very fast
Allegrissimo	faster than Allegro
Vivacissimo	very lively
Prestissimo	as fast as possible

acc.	accompaniment	Dal S.	dal segno
accel.	accelerando	db	decibel
ad lib.	ad libitum	D.C.	da capo
ADSR	envelope generator; initials stand for attack–decay–sustain–release	decresc., decr.	decrescendo
		diap.	diapason
		dim.	diminuendo
affett.	affettuoso	div.	divisi
allarg.	allargando	D.S.	dal segno
all' ott., all' 8va	all' ottava	espr.	espressivo
al seg.	al segno		
AM	amplitude modulation	f	forte
arc.	arcato	ff, fff	fortissimo, fortississimo
arp., arpegg.	arpeggio		
ASCAP	American Society of Composers, Authors, and Publishers	flag.	flageolet
		FM	frequency modulation
		F.O.	full organ
a tem.	a tempo	fp	forte-piano
		fz	forzato, forzando
B.C.	basso continuo		
B.M.I.	Broadcast Music, Inc.	G.P.	general pause; grand positif
brill.	brillante		
BWV	Bach-Werke-Verzeichnis	G.R.	grand recitatif
		graz.	grazioso
c, ©	copyright	Hz	Hertz
c.a.	coll' arco		
Cad.	cadenza	Intro.	introduction
cal.	calando	inv.	inversion
CD	compact disc		
c.d.	colla destra	K.	Köchel
Ch.	choir organ		
c.l.	col legno	leg.	legato
clar.	clarino	legg.	leggiero
Coll' ott., coll' 8va	coll' ottava	L., L.H.	left hand
c.p.	colla parte	M., Man.	Manual
cresc.	crescendo	marc.	marcato
c.s.	colla sinistra	m.d.	mano destra; main droite
c. voc.	colla voce		

mf	mezzo forte	SATB	soprano, alto, tenor, bass (voice parts)
m.g.	main gauche		
M.M.	Maelzel's metronome	scherz.	scherzando
mor.	morendo	Sf, Sfz	sforzando
mp	mezzo piano	Sfp	sforzando-piano
m.s.	mano sinistra; manuscript	sim.	simile
		smorz.	smorzando
m.v.	mezza voce	sos.	sostenuto
		Sp.	Spitze (point)
norm.	normale	s.p.	sul ponticello
		s.t.	sul tasto
obb.	obbligato	stacc.	staccato
op.	opus	stent.	stentando
ord.	ordinario	St. Diap.	stopped diapason
osc.	oscillator	sw.	swell organ
ott.	ottava	Sym.	symphony
p	piano	T.	tasto; tempo; tenor; toe; trill; tutti
P, Ped.	pedal		
perd.	perdendosi	t.c.	tre corde
pes.	pesante	tem.	tempo
pf	pianoforte; piano-forte	ten.	tenuto
pizz.	pizzicato	tr.	trill; treble
pos.	positif	trem.	tremolo
pot.	potentiometer	t.s.	tasto solo
pp	pianissimo		
ppp	pianississimo	u.c.	una corda
		unis.	unison
R.	récit; right hand		
rall.	rallentando	V.	vide; violin; voce; voice; volti
Recit.	recitative		
rf, rfz	rinforzando	Var.	variation
R.H.	right hand	VCA	voltage controlled amplifier
rinf.	rinforzando		
rit., ritard.	ritardando	VCO	voltage controlled oscillator
riten.	ritenuto		
r.s.	rim shot	vibr.	vibrato
		viv.	vivace
S.	segno; sinistra; subito; senza; soprano	v.s.	volti subito

Alt.	Alto (viola)	Klav.	Klavier (piano)
B.Cl.	Bass clarinet	Kl. Fl.	Kleine Flöte (piccolo)
B.D.	Bass drum	Kl. Tr.	Kleine Trommel
Bn., Bsn.	Bassoon		(snare drum)
Br.	Bratsche (viola)		
		Mar.	Marimba
Cb.	Contrabasso		
C.B.	Cow bell	Ob.	Oboe
C.Bsn.	Contrabassoon	Org.	Organ
Cel.	Celesta		
Cemb.	Cembalo	Perc.	Percussion
	(harpsichord)	Pf., Pfte.	Pianoforte (piano)
Cfg.	Contrafagotto	Picc.	Piccolo
	(contrabassoon)	Pk(n).	Pauken (timpani)
Cl.	Clarinet	Pos., Ps.	Posaune (trombone)
Cor.	Cornet	Ptti.	Piatti (cymbals)
Cor. ang.	Cor anglais		
	(English horn)	Sax.	Saxophone
Cor. ingl.	Cor inglese	S.Cym.	Suspended cymbal
	(English horn)	S.D., S.Dr.	Snare drum
Cym.	Cymbal(s)		
		Tamb.	Tambourine
D.B.	Double bass	Tb.	Tuba
Dr.	Drum	Tbn., Trb.	Trombone
		T.D., T.Dr.	Tenor drum
E.H.	English horn	Timb.	Timbales
		Timp.	Timpani
Fag., Fg.	Fagott(o) (bassoon)	Tpt.	Trumpet
Fl.	Flute	Trgl.	Triangle
		Trp.	Trumpet
Gg.	Geige (violin)		
Gr.C.	Gran cassa	Vc., Vcl., Vlc.	Violoncello (cello)
	(bass drum)	Vla.	Viola
		Vl., Vll.	Violins
Haut., Hb.	Hautboy, hoboe (oboe)	Vln(s).	Violin(s)
Hfe.	Harfe (harp)	Vn(s.)	Violin(s)
Hn., Hrn.	Horn (French horn)	Von(s)	Violin(s)
Hps(chd).	Harpsichord	Vv.	Violins
Hrp.	Harp		
		W.B.	Wood block
Kb.	Kontrabass		
	(double bass)	Xyl.	Xylophone
Kl.	Klarinette (clarinet)		

Vowels

ay	hay, weigh
ee	see
ei	kite, height
oh	low, sew, boat
oo, ooh	cool, rule
oy	boy
a	cat
ah	father
au	cow, house
aw	law
o	got, block
e, eh	beg, pen
i	bit, wind
uh	but, nut

Consonants

ch	cheese
g	always hard: green, glad
j	jet
ts	nets
z	zebra, zone
zh	Jacques [zhahk]

Additional German equivalents

u(e)	ü sound. Make "ooh" with lips while pronouncing "ee".
a(e)	ä sound. Sound of "ai" in "fair".
o(e)	ö sound. Say "eh" through closely, rounded lips.
kh	Sound of "h" in whispered "huge". [Bach = Bahkh]

Additional French equivalents

euh	e of father [deux = deuh]
u(e)	French "u" is like "ee" spoken with lips held firmly in a small circle as for whistling.
eu	Like "u" in urge. It is the sound of "eh" spoken with lips firmly rounded on a somewhat larger circle than French "u".
wah	water
y	pronounced like "y" in "yes".
(n)	Indicates that the preceding vowel sound is nasalized: ah(n) oh(n) eu(n) eh(n)

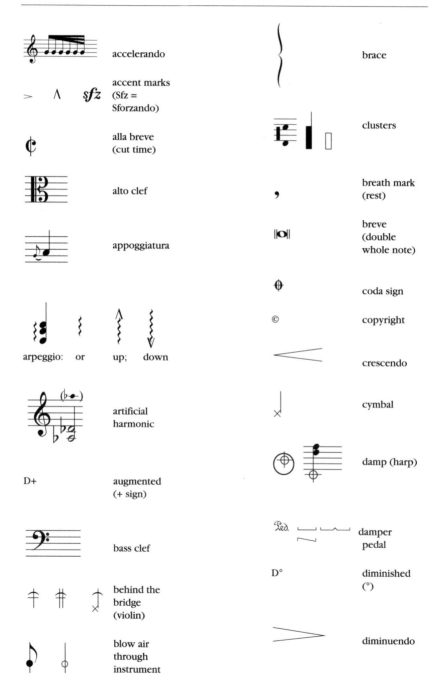

accelerando

accent marks (Sfz = Sforzando)

alla breve (cut time)

alto clef

appoggiatura

arpeggio: or   up;   down

artificial harmonic

D+   augmented (+ sign)

bass clef

behind the bridge (violin)

blow air through instrument

brace

clusters

breath mark (rest)

breve (double whole note)

coda sign

© copyright

crescendo

cymbal

damp (harp)

Ped.   damper pedal

D°   diminished (°)

diminuendo

♭♭	double flat		key signature
𝄪	double sharp		louré bowing
	double, triple tonguing		martelé bowing; hard accent
	double whole rest	M.M. = 60 ♩ = 60	metronome indication
	down-bow		mordent
	fermata		mordent, inverted
	fingernail	+	muted tones (brass); damped cymbal; L.H. pizz.(strings)
𝄴	4/4 meter (common time)	⊙	nail pizzicato
	glissando	○	natural harmonic; open tone
	grace note; acciaccatura		non-arpeggiated (harp, guitar)
U	heel (organ)	8va	ottava (octave)
	highest note possible, lowest note possible	15ma	quindecima (two octaves)
✕ ⊗ ⊗	indeterminate pitches (spoken tones, key slaps, noises)	//	pause

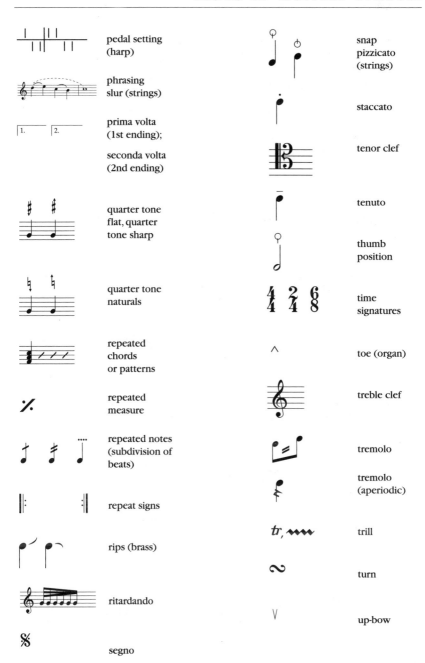

pedal setting (harp)

phrasing slur (strings)

prima volta (1st ending);

seconda volta (2nd ending)

quarter tone flat, quarter tone sharp

quarter tone naturals

repeated chords or patterns

repeated measure

repeated notes (subdivision of beats)

repeat signs

rips (brass)

ritardando

segno

snap pizzicato (strings)

staccato

tenor clef

tenuto

thumb position

time signatures

toe (organ)

treble clef

tremolo

tremolo (aperiodic)

trill

turn

up-bow

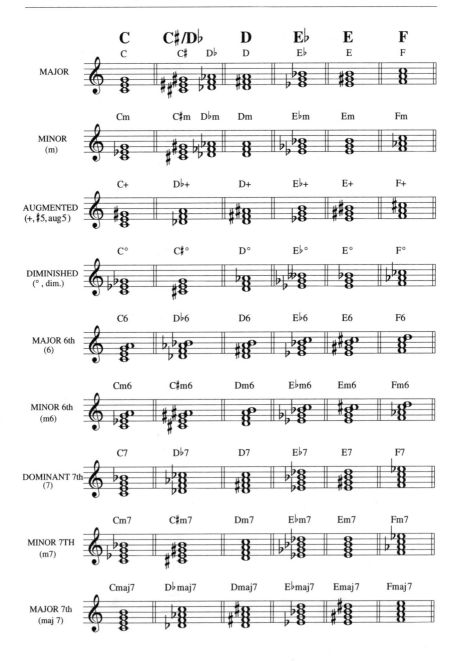

A

A. 1. See *pitch names*. 2. The note used for tuning the orchestra.

a [It., ah] By, for, to, at, in.

ab [G., ahp] Off, referring to organ stops, or mutes.

abdämpfen [G., AHP-damp-fen] To mute.

Abend [G., AH-bent] Evening. *Abendmusik* – evening music.

aber [G., AH-behr] But.

abnehmend [G., AHP-nay-ment] Diminishing.

absolute music Instrumental music which exists for its own sake. The opposite of *program music*, in which visual or poetic (narrative) ideas are presented.

An example of absolute music would be a fugue by Bach; an example of program music is the Pastoral Symphony (No. 6) by Beethoven.

absolute pitch See *perfect pitch*.

abstossen [G., AHP-shtoh-sen] Also *abgestossen*. 1. In violin playing, see *détaché*. 2. In organ music, same as *ab* (off).

abstract music Same as *absolute music*.

a cappella [It., ah kahp-PEHL-lah] Indication for vocal music without instrumental accompaniment.

accelerando [It., ah-chel-er-AHN-doh] Becoming faster. Abbr. as *accel*.

accent Stress or emphasis on a note or chord. Typical accent marks:

acciaccatura [It., ah-chah-kah-TOO-rah] A keyboard ornament, a neighboring tone played at the same time as the principal tone(s), and then released immediately. Example B shows how the acciaccatura – Example A – is actually played:

Ex. A   Ex. B

Also notated:

accidentals Sharps, flats, and natural signs used to indicate or cancel chromatic alterations. (See *flat*, *natural*, *pitch names*, *sharp*.)

accolade [F., a-kuh-LAHD] Brace.

accompaniment The musical background for a principal part. This background may be the left hand of a keyboard composition, the orchestral background for a soloist, etc.

accord [F., a-KUHR] 1. Chord. 2. Manner of tuning, esp. the lute and other similar instruments.

accordatura [It., ah-kohr-dah-TOO-rah] See *accord (2)*.

accordion A hand-held musical instrument consisting of two headboards connected by folding bellows. The air produced by the bellows activates vibrating metal reeds.

The modern accordion has a keyboard on the right side for melody notes, and buttons on the left side for bass notes and chords.

accordo [It., ahk-KOHR-doh] Chord.

accusé (F., a-ku(e)-ZAY] With emphasis.

acht [G., akht] Eight.

Achtel [G., AKH-tel] Eighth note. *achtel Pause* – eighth rest. See *notes*.

acoustics 1. The science which studies the production, transmission, and reception of sound. 2. The properties of a room (or concert hall) which affect the quality of sounds being transmitted.

action The mechanism of a keyboard instrument which transmits the motion of fingers to the strings.

The action of the harp, controlled by the feet, is responsible for raising or lowering the pitch of the strings (either a half step or a whole step).

adagietto [It., ah-dah-jee-EHT-toh] 1. A tempo somewhat faster and lighter than *adagio*. 2. A composition in the tempo of *adagietto*.

adagio [It., ah-DAH-jyoh] 1. A slow tempo between *lento* and *andante*. *adagio assai* – very slow. 2. A slow composition, often the slow movement

of a *sonata* or *symphony*.

adagissimo [It., ah-dah-JEE-see-moh] Very slow.

added sixth 1. The sixth added to a triad. 2. A chord, major or minor, to which a sixth has been added, e.g., C-E-G-A, C-E-G-A♭.

additive synthesis Combining sine waves to create more complex tones.

à demi voix [F., a deuh-mee VWAH] At half voice; same as *sotto voce*.

à deux [F., a DEUH] For two instruments or voices.

à deux mains [F., a deuh MEH(N)] For two hands.

ad libitum [L., ahd LEE-bee-toom] Abbr. *ad lib.* Freely, allowing the performer to vary the tempo or improvise.

ADSR See *envelope generator; electronic music*.

a due [It., ah DOO-ay] 1. In orchestral parts, a direction for two instruments notated on one staff to play in unison. 2. With strings, an indication to play *divisi*.

Aeolian harp An ancient instrument consisting of a box with strings stretched over two bridges. When exposed to a current of air, it produces varying harmonic sounds.

Aeolian mode See *Gregorian chant III*.

aerophones See *instruments*.

affabile [It., ahf-FAH-bee-lay] Gentle, pleasing.

affannato, affannoso (It., ahf-fahn-NAH-toh, ahf-fahn-NOH-soh] Panting, excited.

affettuoso [It., ahf-fet-too-OH-soh] Affectionately. Abbr. *affett.*

aftertouch Pressure applied to a key after it is struck, which sends additional MIDI data. Also see *electronic music*.

agevole [It., ah-JEH-voh-lay] Lightly, easily.

agitato [It., ah-jee-TAH-toh] Agitated, excited.

Agnus Dei [L.,AHN-yoos DAY-ee] "Lamb of God" – See *Mass*.

agogic An accent produced by a longer duration rather than by an increase in loudness.

agréments [F., a-gray-MAH(N)] Ornaments.

air A tune or melody. The term *air* was commonly used in the 17th and 18th centuries.

Ais [G., AH-ees] The note A sharp. See *pitch names*.

Akkord [G., ah-KOHRT] Chord.

al [It., ahl]; **à la** [F., a la] To the; at the.

Alberti bass An accompaniment pattern consisting of broken chords in the pattern: lowest, highest, middle, highest.

album leaf A short, simple piece.

al Coda [It., ahl KOH-dah] To the Coda.

al fine [It., ahl FEE-nay] To the end.

aleatory music Music in which chance or improvisation is an essential element. Aleatory music (also called *chance music*) became important after 1945 and has been used extensively by such composers as John Cage, Earle Brown, Morton Feldman, and Karlheinz Stockhausen.

alla, all' [It., AHL-lah]; **à la, à l'** [F., a la] In the manner of, e.g., *rondo alla Turca* – rondo in the Turkish style.

alla breve [It., ahl-lah BREH-vay] A time signature ¢ indicating two often quick beats per measure with the half note receiving one beat (2/2). Also known as *cut time*.

allargando [It., ahl-lahr-GAHN-doh] Abbr. *allarg.* Gradually slower (and often louder).

allegretto [It., ahl-leh-GREHT-toh] 1. A little slower than *allegro*. 2. A piece in the tempo of allegretto.

allegro [It., ahl-LEH-groh] Fast tempo or movement. *allegro con brio* – fast and with spirit; *allegro con moto* – fast, with motion; *allegro ma non troppo* – fast, but not too much so; *allegro molto* – very fast; *allegro vivace* – fast and vivacious.

alle [G., AH-leh] All, as in *alle Instrumente* – all instruments.

alleluia (Greek, ahl-lay-LOO-yah] An exclamation of praise, derived from the Hebrew *hallelujah*.

Alleluia See *Mass*.

allemande [F., al-MAH(N)D] A dance in moderate 2/4 or 4/4 meter. In keyboard music, the allemande is the first movement in a baroque suite; it is in binary form. Also see *suite*.

allentando [It., ahl-len-TAHN-doh] Slowing down.

allmählich [G., AHL-ma(e)-likh] Gradually.

all' ottava [It., ahl oht-TAH-vah] Play an octave higher than written.

all' unisono [It., ahl ooh-nee-SOH-noh] In unison (or octaves).

al segno [It., ahl SEH-nyoh] To the sign ※.

alt 1. Term for the high notes G to F

which are said to be "in alt." 2. (G.) The second highest member of an instrumental or vocal family: *Altklarinette* – alto clarinet.

alternativo [It., ahl-ter-nah-TEE-voh], **alternativement** [F., al-tehr-na-teev-MAH(N)] Alternating one section with another, i.e., with a pair of like dances, the first is repeated after the second.

alto (F.) Viola.

alto [It.,AHL-toh] Low female voices.

alto clarinet The alto clarinet is larger than the B♭ clarinet, and it has a lower range. It is also called the E♭ alto clarinet, since it is pitched in E♭. Its range extends a perfect fifth below the B♭ clarinet.

alto clef See *clef.*

alto flute A larger, lower-pitched version of the orchestral flute. It has the same written range but sounds a perfect fourth lower (pitched in G).

alto saxophone See *saxophone.*

amabile [It., ah-MAH-bee-lay] Amiably, charming.

âme [F., ahm] Sound post of an instrument in the violin or viol family.

amen Hebrew: "So be it." Often appears at the close of a hymn, psalm, or other sacred music.

am Frosch [G., ahm FROHSH] "At the frog." Direction to use the part of the bow nearest the hand.

am Griffbrett [G., ahm GRIF-bret] "On the fingerboard." Bowing near the fingerboard (sul tasto).

amore, con [It., ah-MOH-ray] With love, affection.

amorevole [It., ah-moh-REH-voh-lay] Loving.

amoroso [It., ah-moh-ROH-soh] Amorous, loving.

amplifier A device used to increase the power or voltage of a signal.

amplitude The maximum value of power during a single cycle of a wave.

amplitude modulation In *electronic music,* a periodic fluctuation in loudness. See electronic music.

am Steg [G., ahm SHTEHK] "At the bridge." Bowing near the bridge (sul ponticello).

an [G., ahn] On; to.

anacrusis Upbeat, or pick-up.

analog Refers to circuits that produce a continuously fluctuating electrical signal. With a digital circuit, data expressed by numbers is used to produce signal changes. Also see electronic music.

analog music synthesis See electronic music.

anche [F., ah(n)sh] Reed, esp. the reed stops of the organ (anches).

ancia [It.,AHN-chee-ah] Reed.

ancora [It., ahng-KOH-rah] Once more; yet. *ancora più forte* – still louder.

andante [It., ahn-DAHN-tay] A moderate tempo or movement, at a walking pace.

andantino [It., ahn-dahn-TEE-noh] A little faster than andante. However, the literal meaning is just the opposite.

Anfang [G.,AHN-fahng] Beginning. *vom Anfang* – from the beginning (da capo).

Anhang [G., AHN-hang] A coda, a postscript.

anima, con [It.,AH-nee-mah] With spirit.

animato [It., ah-nee-MAH-toh]; **animé** [F., a-nee-MAY]; **animoso** [It., ah-nee-MOH-soh] Animated, lively.

anlaufen [G., AHN-lau-fen] To increase in volume.

anmutig [G.,AHN-moo-tikh] Gracefully.

Ansatz [G., AHN-zahts] 1. In wind playing, adjustment of the embouchure. 2. Attack.

Anschlag [G., AHN-shlahg] 1. In piano playing, touch. 2. A double grace note, played on the beat.

anschwellen [G., AHN-shvel-len] Crescendo.

answer See *fugue.*

antecedent and consequent These terms usually refer to musical phrases, where a question (antecedent) is immediately followed by its answer (consequent).

anthem A sacred choral composition of the Protestant church, sung in English.

anticipation See *nonharmonic tones I (3).*

antico [It., ahn-TEE-koh] Ancient, old.

antike Zimbeln [G., ahn-TEE-keh TSIM-beln] See *crotales.*

antiphonal Referring to music in which there are two or more alternating groups.

antique cymbals Crotales.

Antwort [G., AHNT-vohrt] Answer, as in fugues.

anwachsend [G., AHN-vahk-sent] Swelling, increasing.

aperto [It., ah-PEHR-toh] Open.

a piacere [It., ah pyah-CHAY-ray] "At pleasure," esp. with regard to tempo and rhythm.

a poco [It., ah POH-koh] A little; gradually.

a poco a poco [It., ah POH-koh ah POH-koh) Little by little.

appassionato [It., ahp-pahs-syoh-NAH-toh] Passionately.

appoggiatura [It., ahp-poh-jah-TOO-rah] A nonharmonic tone, usually written as a small note without a slash, which is usually played on the beat. Its resolution time varies considerably, depending upon the style and context in which it occurs. Also see *nonharmonic tones (II).*

a punta d'arco [It., ah poon-tah DAHR-koh] With the point of the bow.

à quatre mains [F., a katr-MEH(N)] For four hands.

arabesque (F.) 1. Title used for compositions by Schumann, Debussy, and others. 2. Ornamentation or embellishment of a melody.

arcato [It., ahr-KAH-toh] Bowed.

archet [F., ar-SHEH], **arco** [It., AHR-koh] Bow (of the violin, etc.). In string parts, *arco* is used to cancel a *pizzicato* (plucked) indication.

ardente [It., ahr-DEN-tay] With fire.

ardito [It., ahr-DEE-toh] Bold.

ardore, con [It., ahr-DOH-ray] With ardor, warmth.

aria [It., AH-ree-ah] An elaborate setting of a song for one (or two) voices, with instrumental accompaniment. The aria is prominent in cantatas, oratorios, and operas.

aria buffa [It., AH-ree-ah BOOF-fah] A comic or humorous aria.

arietta [It., ah-ree-EHT-tah] A short aria.

arioso [It., ah-ree-OH-soh] Like an aria. Lyrical and expressive.

armonioso [It., ahr-moh-NYOH-soh] Harmoniously.

armure [F., ar-MU(E)R] Key signature.

arpa [It., Sp.,AHR-pah] Harp.

arpeggiator An electronic device which automatically arpeggiates (rolls) the notes of a chord.

arpeggio 1. In the style of a harp: the notes of a chord played consecutively instead of simultaneously (Ex. A).

In keyboard and guitar music, arpeggiation may be indicated by a vertical wavy line placed before the chord (Ex. B).

Ex. A

Ex. B

2. See *bowing (9)*.

arrangement Adaptation of a composition for instruments other than those for which it was intended originally; for example, an arrangement of Beethoven's *Für Elise* (piano solo) for string quartet.

arsis [Gr.,AHR-sis] Upbeat.

articolato [It., ahr-tee-koh-LAH-toh] Articulated.

articulation Clear and effective execution, with respect to breathing, attack, legato, staccato, etc.

artificial harmonics See *harmonics (2)*.

art song A professionally-composed song written in a classical style, as opposed to a folk or popular song. The term mainly refers to 19th-century settings of poetry sung with piano accompaniment.

As [G., ahs] The note A flat. See *pitch names*.

ASCAP American Society of Composers, Authors, and Publishers. Address: 1 Lincoln Plaza, New York, N.Y. 10023

assai [It., ah-SAHee] Very, much (or rather). *allegro assai* – quite fast.

assez [F., a-SAY] Enough; rather.

Atem [G.,AH-tehm] Breath.

a tempo [It., ah TEHM-poh] Return to regular tempo, esp. after a *ritardando*.

atonality Music which does not have a tonal center; the avoidance of tonality. Twelve-tone music is atonal; however, the terms are not synonymous.

Much of the classical music of the 20th century is atonal. Also see *serial music*.

attacca [It., aht-TAHK-kah] Begin the next movement or section without pause.

attack 1. The audible beginning of a musical note or phrase. 2. In electronic music, the amplitude characteristics at the initiation of a sound. See *electronic music*.

attenuator device used to adjust the amplitude of a signal (volume control).

aubade [F., oh-BAHD] Morning music.

au chevalet See *bowing (special effects – 1)*.

audio 1. Relating to frequencies which can be heard (audible), approx. 15 cycles per second to 20,000 cycles per second. 2. Relating to sound reproduction, as distinct from *video*.

auf [G., auf] On, upon, in at.

aufgeregt [G., AUF-geh-rehkt] Excited, agitated.

aufgeweckt [G., AUF-geh-vehkt] Bright, lively.

Aufstrich [G.,AUF-strikh] Upbow.

Auftakt [G.,AUF-tahkt] Upbeat.

augmentation An increase in the duration of the notes of a phrase or melody. The notes may be doubled in value, or even tripled or quadrupled. Also see *diminution*.

A)

B) Augmentation of A

augmented interval An interval which is one half-step larger than a perfect or major interval. Also see *interval*.

augmented sixth chord See *sixth chords*.

augmented triad A major triad with a raised fifth. See *triad*.

ausdrucksvoll [G., AUS-drooks-fohl] Full of expression.

Ausgabe [G., AUS-gah-beh] Edition.

authentic cadence See *cadence*.

authentic mode See *Gregorian chant*.

autoharp An instrument of the zither family.

auxiliary tone, auxiliary note See *nonharmonic tones I (2)*.

avec [F., a-VEHK] With.

Ave Maria [L., AH-vay mah-REE-ah] "Hail, Mary." A hymn or prayer to the Virgin Mary.

B

B. 1. See *pitch names*. 2. In German, *B* stands for B flat.

bacchetta [It., bah-KET-tah] Drumstick.

Bach-Gesellschaft [G., BAHKH-geh-zehl-shahft] Bach Society, founded in 1850 at the centenary of the death of J. S. Bach. The Society published a complete critical edition of his works. In 1900 a new Society was formed (Neue Bach Gesellschaft).

Bach-Werke-Verzeichnis [G., BAHKH-vehr-keh fehr-TSEIKH-nis] The thematic catalogue of the works of J. S. Bach, first published by the *Bach-Gesellschaft*.

backbeat Offbeat; in jazz, accented second and fourth beats in 4/4 time.

badinage [F., ba-dee-NAZH] A dance-like piece in a playful style, generally for piano.

bagatelle [F., ba-ga-TEHL] "Trifle." A short, usually easy, piece of music.

bagpipe Ancient instrument, now common in Scotland, with pipes connected to a wind bag. Each *drone* pipe produces a continuous one-note accompaniment, while a *chanter* pipe equipped with sound holes produces melody notes.

balalaika [Russ., bahl-eh-LEI-kah] A triangular-shaped Russian instrument of the guitar family, with three strings tuned in fourths.

ballad 1. A simple narrative song. 2. In popular music, the term is used loosely by musicians to describe slow lyrical songs, esp. instrumental jazz pieces.

ballade [F., ba-LAD] Fourteenth and fifteenth-century poetic/musical form, used extensively by the composer Machaut.

Ballade [G., bah-LAH-deh] The German use of the term *ballade* refers to a poem derived from English ballads, usually dealing with medieval subjects. The poet Goethe (1749-1832) wrote such poems, which were often set to music.

The term also was used by both Chopin and Brahms for several of their large piano works in narrative style.

ballad opera Type of 18th-century English opera, consisting of spoken dialogue alternating with simple songs (ballads). Also see *opera*.

ballata [It., bahl-LAH-tah] Fourteenth-century Italian poetic/musical form, consisting of three stanzas that alternate with the refrain.

ballet [F., ba-LEH]; **Ballett** [G., bah-LET] A theatrical performance by dancers, with instrumental accompaniment, in which the motion of the dancers tells a story or depicts a mood.

balletto [It., bahl-LET-toh] A dance-like vocal composition of ca. 1600.

ballo [It., BAHL-loh] 1. Generic term for dance. 2. Since the 15th-century, the term has been used to denote dances and works in ballet style. 3. *Balletto*.

band 1. Ensemble, combo. 2. Acoustics: a specific range of frequencies.

band pass filter In electronic music, a filter that allows only a selective frequency band to be transmitted. See *electronic music*.

band reject filter In electronic music, a filter which eliminates specific frequencies and lets all others through. See *electronic music*.

banjo A stringed, fretted instrument with a long neck and a drum-like body. The banjo is a common instrument in Dixieland and bluegrass music.

bar A vertical line which divides the staff or staves into *measures*.

A *double bar* is placed between sections or at the end of a piece.

barcarole; barcarolle [F., bar-ka-RUHL] A Venetian boat song, in 6/8 or 12/8 meter, with a rocking rhythm.

baritone; baryton [F., ba-ree-TOH(N)], **Bariton** [G., BAH-ree-tohn] See *voices, range of.*

baritone horn Brass instrument similar to a tuba, but smaller.

baritone saxophone See *saxophone.*

baroque See *History of Western Music.*

barré [F., ba-RAY] In lute and guitar playing, stopping some or all of the strings by holding the forefinger across them.

baryton String instrument similar to the viola da gamba; not in general use today.

bass 1. See *voices, range of.* 2. Double bass (G.).

bass clarinet See *Woodwind Instruments (6).*

bass clef See *clef.*

bass drum See *Percussion Instruments (10).*

bass guitar Also called *electric bass.* Electrically amplified four-string guitar with a low range. The electric bass is an essential part of the modern rock band, and it is also common in jazz groups as a replacement for the double bass.

Bassklarinette [G., BAHS-klah-ree-net-teh] Bass clarinet.

basso [It., BAHS-soh] 1. Bass. 2. Bass singer.

basso continuo [It., bahs-soh kohn-TEE-noo-oh] See *thoroughbass.*

bassoon; basson [F., ba-SOH(N)] See *Woodwind Instruments (7).*

basso ostinato [It., bahs-soh ohs-tee-NAH-toh] See *ground bass.*

Bassposaune [G., BAHS-poh-zau-neh] Bass trombone.

bass trombone See *Brass Instruments (4).*

Basstuba [G., BAHS-too-bah] Tuba.

baton, bâton [F., ba-TOH(N)] The conductor's stick.

batterie [F., ba-TREE] 1. The percussion group of the orchestra. 2. A drum roll. 3. Striking the strings of the guitar. 4. In baroque music, arpeggiated passages, or arpeggiation of passages notated as chords.

battuta [It., baht-TOO-tah] 1. Beat. 2. The strong beat at the beginning of a measure. *a battuta* – return to strict time.

B dur [G., BAY duhr] B-flat major.

Be [G., bay] The flat sign (♭).

beam See *notes.*

beat 1. The basic unit of musical time; pulse. 2. A frequency pulsation resulting from the interference of two slightly different frequencies, for instance, two piano strings tuned to the same pitch but slightly out of tune with each other. Beats are crucial to tuning.

bebop See *bop.*

Bebung [G., BAY-boong] A type of vibrato that can be produced on the clavichord by moving a finger sideways on a depressed key.

Notated:

bec [F., behk] The mouthpiece of the clarinet or recorder.

bécarre [F., bay-KAR] The natural sign (♮).

Becken [G., BEHK-en] Cymbals.

bedächtig [G., beh-DEHKH-tikh] Deliberate; thoughtfully.

Begleitung [G., beh-GLEI-toong(k)] Accompaniment.

bel canto [It., bel KAHN-toh] "Beautiful song" – the Italian singing style of the 18th century, which emphasizes the beauty of sound and technical facility.

belebend, belebt [G., beh-LAY-bent, beh-LAYPT] Animated, lively.

bell 1. The flared opening of a wind instrument, esp. brass. 2. Any of a variety of hollow, metal percussion instruments.

bell choir Group performing with specially tuned bells, on which melodies as well as accompaniments can be played.

bellicoso [It., behl-lee-KOH-soh] Bellicose; martial.

bell-lyra, bell lyre Portable *glockenspiel* used in marching bands.

bells Chimes. See *Percussion Instruments – 6.*

bémol [F., bay-MUHL]; **bemolle** [It., bay-MAHL-lay] The flat sign (♭).

ben(e) [It., BEH-nay] Well, good.

benediction 1. A short blessing which concludes a religious service. 2. (Cap.) A Catholic devotion.

Benedictus [L., bay-nay-DEEK-toos] 1. A canticle of the Roman Catholic Church. 2. Second part of the Sanctus of a Mass.

ben marcato [It., ben mahr-KAH-toh] Well and clearly marked.

bequadro [It., beh-KWAH-droh] The natural sign (♮).

berceuse [F., behr-SEUHZ] Lullaby.

bergamasca [It., behr-gah-MAH-skah] A dance-like composition suggesting Italian peasant life, the term being derived from the district of Bergamo in northern Italy.

beruhigt, beruhigend [G., beh-ROO-eegt, be-ROO-ee-gent] Calm, quiet.

Bes [G., behs] The note B double flat. See *pitch names.*

beschleunigt [G., beh-SHLOY-nikt] Accelerando.

Besetzung [G., beh-ZETS-oong] Setting; the instruments used in a composition.

bestimmt [G., beh-SHTIMT] With decision.

betont [G., beh-TOHNT] Stressed, emphasized.

bewegt [G., beh-VEHKT] Animated; *con moto.*

bianca [It., bee-AHN-kah] Half note. See *notes.*

binary form and **ternary form** *binary form* – A musical form consisting of two contrasting sections, each repeated (AABB). Example: the Allemande of a Bach suite. *ternary form* – Follows the scheme ABA (song form). Example: Beethoven, Piano Sonata No. 7, second movement.

bind See *tie.*

bis [F., bees] Twice, repeated; e.g., encore.

bisbigliando [It, bees-bee-LYAHN-doh] Harp tremolo effect obtained by a quickly repeated finger motion on two (sets of) enharmonically equivalent strings.

biscroma [It., bees-KROH-mah] Thirty-second note. See *notes.*

bisdiapason (L.) The interval or range of two octaves.

bitonality The simultaneous use of two chords or keys. This technique has been used by several 20th-century composers, notably Stravinsky and Milhaud.

blanche [F., blah(n)sh] Half note. See *notes.*

Blasinstrument [G., BLAHZ-in-stroo-ment] Wind instrument. *Blasmusik* – wind music.

Blech [G., blekh] Brass; e.g., *Blech-instrumente.*

Blockflöte [G., BLOK-flo(e)-teh] Recorder. See *recorder.*

blues A type of popular music originating in the U.S.A. in the early 1900's. The roots of the blues appear to lie in African-American spirituals and work songs. Later, ragtime had an influence; however, blues songs are generally slower.

Two characteristics of the blues are: 1) Repeated 12-measure phrases improvised on the chord progression I-I-I-I-IV-IV-I-I-V-IV-I-I . (Substitute chords are common, and the use of dominant seventh chords is traditional.) 2) The use of flatted (blue) notes in a scale:

BMI Broadcast Music, Inc. Address: 320 W. 57th St., New York, NY 10019

B moll [G., BAY mohl] B flat minor.

bocca [It., BOHK-kah] Mouth. *bocca chiusa* – With closed mouth; humming.

Bogen [G., BOH-gen] 1. The bow of a violin. 2. Tie. (See *tie.*)

bois [F., bwah] "Wood." *Les bois:* The woodwinds.

bolero [Sp., boh-LEH-roh] 1. A lively Spanish dance in 3/4 meter. 2. A Cuban dance in 2/4 meter.

bombarda [It., bohm-BAHR-dah]; **bombarde** [F., boh(m)-BAHRD] 1. (Bass) shawm. 2. An organ stop of the reed family, usually of 32- or 16-foot pitch.

Bombardon [G., BOM-bahr-don] The German equivalent of the *helicon.*

bongos A pair of small one-headed drums, open at the bottom. Played with the fingers.

boogie-woogie A style of blues piano characterized by left hand patterns such as:

bop Mid-20th-century jazz pioneered by such musicians as Dizzie Gillespie, Miles Davis, and Charlie Parker. Bop tends to sound dissonant and complex; tempos are sometimes extremely fast. Bop's influence on jazz has been profound, since it is often thought of as "pure" jazz. Also known as bebop, or rebop.

Bordun [G., bohr-DOON]; **bordone** [It., bohr-DOH-nay] See *bourdon.*

bore The interior cavity or diameter of a wind instrument, either *straight* (trumpet, flute, etc.) or *conical* (oboe, saxophone, etc.).

bouché [F., boo-SHAY] 1. Winds: muted. 2. Organ pipes: stopped.

bouche fermée [F., boo-SHAY fehr-MAY] With closed mouth; humming.

bouffe [F., boof] Comic.

bourdon [F., boor-DOH(N)] 1. Drone bass. 2. An organ flute stop of capped or stopped pipes.

bourrée [F., boo-RAY] A 17th-century French dance in quick duple meter. The bourrée is a movement in some suites of J. S. Bach. Also see *suite*.

bow Used to play the instruments of the violin family. A bow consists of a rod on which horse hair (or a substitute material) is stretched.

BOWING

The technique of using a bow.

1. Legato [It., leh-GAH-toh] Groups of notes are slurred together or indicated by:

a) Up-bow Moving in the direction from tip of bow to frog.

b) Down-bow Moving in the direction from frog of bow to tip.

2. Détaché [F., day-ta-SHAY] Each note is bowed separately. *détaché*

3. Martelé [F., mar-teuh-LAY] "Hammered" stroke – a broad, clearly articulated stroke.

4. Sautillé [F., soh-tee-YAY] A very fast spiccato.

5. Spiccato [It., speek-KAH-toh] The bow bounces off the string; each note is played with a separate bow stroke.

6. Jeté [F., zheuh-TAY] (more commonly *ricochet*) "Throwing" the bow so that it bounces to produce several notes on the same bow stroke.

7. Louré [F., loo-RAY], **portato** [It., pohr-TAH-toh] Used to effect a slight separation within one bow stroke.

8. Slurred staccato On-the-string bowing – each note gets a separate articulation in the same stroke.

9. Arpeggio [It., ahr-PEH-jyoh] Broken chords where each tone is on a different string; sometimes the bow is bounced (similar to *ricochet*).

10. Tremolo [It., TREH-moh-loh} Rapid strokes on one note or between two notes in an interval.

Bowing special effects:

1. Sul ponticello [It., sool pohn-tee-CHEHL-loh], **au chevalet** [F., oh sheuh-va-LEH], **am steg** [G., ahm STEHK] Bow near the bridge, a glassy, ethereal effect.

2. Sul tasto, sulla tastiera [It., sool TAHS-toh, sool-lah tas-TYEH-rah], **sur la touche** [F., su(e) la TOOSH, **am Griff-brett** [G., ahm GRIF-bret] (also *flautando*) Bow over the fingerboard, a soft flute-like effect.

3. Col legno [It., kohl LEH-nyoh] With the wood of the bow, a percussive effect.

brace Bracket used to join two or more staffs (staves), forming a "system."

BRASS INSTRUMENTS

Below is a description of each instrument and its range.

1. **Horn** (French horn). A long conical tube coiled into circles, ending in a large flaring bell. The horn has three rotary valves; it is tuned in F.

sounds a P5 lower

2. **Trumpet** Has a predominantly cylindrical bore and three piston valves. The trumpet has a brilliant, penetrating tone; it is tuned in B♭. C trumpets are commonly used in the orchestra – they sound as written.

sounds a M2 lower

3. **Trombone** (tenor trombone) Has a predominantly straight bore, a cup-shaped mouthpiece, and a slide instead of valves. The slide enables the trombonist to execute a glissando, but usually this feature is reserved for special effects.

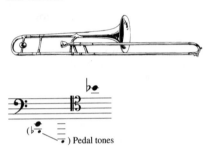

) Pedal tones

sounds as written

4. **Bass trombone, tenor-bass trombone** The bass trombone, tuned in F, has been replaced by the tenor-bass trombone, which has the size and pitch of a tenor trombone but the bore of a bass trombone. A single valve lowers the pitch a perfect fourth to that of the bass trombone. As with the tenor trombone, pedals are commonly used below the given range.

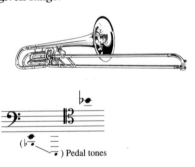

) Pedal tones

sounds as written

5. Tuba The largest brass instrument, the tuba comes in a variety of sizes and shapes. It has 3 to 5 piston valves, a conical bore, and a large flaring bell.

sounds as written

Bratsche [G., BRAHT-sheh] Viola.

bravo [It., BRAH-voh] Excellent, very good. (For a female performer, the correct term is "brava.")

bravura [It., brah-VOO-rah] Boldness, brilliance.

breit [G., breit] Broad, *largo*.

breve [L., BREH-veh, brev] Double whole note. ‖O‖

bridge For string instruments, the wooden support over which the strings are stretched.

bridge passage A musical passage which serves to connect two themes or sections.

brillant [F., bree-YAH(N)]; **brillante** [It., breel-YAHN-tay] Brilliant.

brindisi [It., breen-DEE-see] Drinking song, esp. in operas.

brio [It., BREE-oh] Vigor, spirit.

brioso [It., bree-OH-soh] Vigorously.

brisé [F., bree-ZAY] Arpeggio playing; detached bowing.

broken chord See *arpeggio (1)*.

broken octave Octave in which the notes are sounded separately, or played *tremolo*.

brumeux [F., bru(e)-MEUH] "Misty"; veiled.

Brummstimmen [G., BROOM-shtimmen] Humming.

buffo [It., BOOF-foh] Comic; comic character in an opera.

bugle A military brass instrument without valves.

Bühne [G.), BU(E)H-neh] Stage.

burla, burlesca [It., BOOR-lah, boor-LEH-skah] A playful composition.

burlando [It., boor-LAHN-doh] Facetious, comical.

burlesque [F., bu(e)r-LEHSK] "Ludicrous." Stage entertainment of a comic and earthy character.

C

C. 1. See *pitch names*. 2. Time signature for common time (4/4 meter).

cabaletta [It., kah-bah-LET-tah] A short, rather plain, operatic song.

caccia [It., KAHT-chah] A 14th-century canonic form dealing with hunting, fishing, etc.

cachucha [Sp., kah-CHOO-chah] Spanish dance in triple meter, similar to the *bolero*.

cacophony Harshness; discord.

cadence 1. Two (or more) chords in succession which conclude a section or a composition. The following are various cadence formulas:

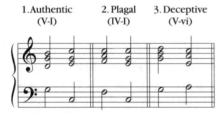

1. Authentic (V-I) 2. Plagal (IV-I) 3. Deceptive (V-vi)

A *perfect cadence* ends on the I chord and contains the tonic note in the soprano; therefore Ex. 1 above is a *perfect authentic cadence*.

Cadences prior to the baroque period differ substantially from those just described.

2. Drum beat routines used by marching bands.

cadenza [It., kah-DEN-zah] A brilliant solo passage, either improvisational or written-out, inserted near the end of a composition, esp. the first movement of a *concerto*.

caisse claire [F., kehs KLEHR] Snare drum.

caisse roulante [F., cehs roo-LAH(N)T] Tenor drum.

calando [It., kah-LAHN-doh] Becoming quieter.

calcando [It., kahl-KAHN-doh] Hurrying the tempo.

calliope [kah-LEI-oh-pee] A large keyboard instrument consisting of steam-blown whistles.

calmo [It., KAHL-moh] Calm, tranquil.

calore, con [It., kah-LOH-ray] With warmth.

calypso A type of Caribbean song, highly syncopated and repetitious.

cambia, cambiano [It., KAHM-byah, KAHM-byah-noh] Orchestral direction to change instruments or tuning.

cambiata See *nonharmonic tones I (4)*.

camera, musica da [It., MOO-see-kah dah KAH-meh-rah] Chamber music.

campana [It., kahm-PAH-nah] Bell. *campanella* – "little bell"; glockenspiel.

campana tubolare, campane [It., kahm-PAH-nah too-boh-LAH-ray, kahm-PAH-nay] Chimes.

cancel Natural sign (♮).

canción [Sp., kahn-see-OHN] Song.

cancrizans See *retrograde*.

canon 1. A contrapuntal device where one voice exactly imitates another, although not necessarily at the same pitch. 2. A composition which uses *canon*.

canonic imitation See *imitation*; *canon*.

cantabile [It., kahn-TAH-bee-lay] Singable, in a singing style.

cantata A vocal composition based on a narrative text, consisting of several movements such as arias, recitatives, duets, and choruses.

canticle (from L.) 1. A liturgical text similar to a Psalm. 2. A liturgical song.

cantilena [It., kahn-tee-LAY-nah] A song or passage with a lyrical character.

cantique [F., kah(n)-TEEK] Canticle.

canto [It., KAHN-toh] 1. Song, melody. 2. A soprano part.

cantor Soloist or chanter in a religious service.

cantus firmus [L., KAHN-toos FEER-moos] An existing melody that is used as the basis of a contrapuntal (usually vocal) composition. The cantus firmus usually appears unchanged in the tenor voice, in contrast with other voices, which are more florid.

canzona, canzone [It., kahn-ZOH-nah, kahn-ZOH-nay] 1. A lyrical song. 2. A type of 16th-century secular vocal music. 3. An instrumental work which was a predecessor to the sonata and the fugue.

canzonet, canzonetta [It., kahn-zoh-NET, kahn-zoh-NET-tah] A short, dance-like song, esp. of the 16th and 17th-centuries.

capo [It., KAH-poh] 1. Head; beginning. See *da capo*. 2. Short for *capotasto (2)*.

capotasto [It., kah-poh-TAHS-toh] 1. The nut of stringed instruments. 2. A clamping device which is used to shorten the vibrating length of guitar or lute strings.

cappella [It., kahp-PEHL-lah] 1. Chapel. 2. See *a cappella*.

capriccio [It., kah-PREET-chyoh] A short, humorous keyboard piece, esp. of the 17th-18th centuries.

carillon 1. A chromatic set of bells hung in a tower and played by a keyboard. 2. Composition for a carillon. 3. Glockenspiel.

carol A traditional Christmas song.

carrée [F., ka-RAY] Breve. See *breve*.

cassa [It., KAHS-sah] Drum.

castanets A percussion instrument made of two wooden shells that are clicked together. Castanets are used to accompany Spanish dances and as a coloristic effect in instrumental music.

catch An English *round*, 17th-18th centuries.

cavatina [It., kah-vah-TEE-nah] An operatic solo, shorter and simpler than an aria.

C clef See *clef*.

cédez [F., say-DAY] Slow down.

celere [It., CHEH-leh-reh] Rapid.

celesta (keyboard glockenspiel). An instrument resembling a small upright piano. Steel bars are struck by hammers connected to the keyboard action. It has a delicate, "watery" tone.

sounds 1 octave higher

celeste Organ stop with two ranks of pipes, one mistuned slightly to create an undulating sound.

cello See *Violin Family (3)*.

Cembalo [G., TSHEHM-bah-loh; **[clavi] cembalo** [It., (klah-vee) CHEM-bah-loh] Harpsichord.

cent A unit of measuring musical intervals, equal to 1/100 of a semitone (half step).

Ces [G., tsehs] C flat. See *pitch names*.

chaconne [F., sha-KUHN] A variation form based on a regularly repeated chord progression.

chalumeau [F., sha-lu(e)-MOH] The lowest register of the clarinet.

chamber music Music for small groups, where each player has a separate part.

chance music See *aleatory music*.

channel Pathways used to transmit and receive MIDI data. See *electronic music*.

chanson [F., shah(n)-SOH(N)] 1. The French word for song. 2. In the 15th and 16th centuries, the chanson was an important type of vocal composition, often contrapuntal in style.

chant 1. See *plainsong, Gregorian chant*. 2. Any kind of semi-spoken singing, i.e., recitation on a single tone.

chanter See *bagpipe*.

chantey, chanty Work song of English and American sailors, sung while pulling ropes, etc.

character piece A short 19th-century (piano) composition, depicting a scene, mood, person, etc.

chasse [F., shas] Hunt; chase.

che [It., kay] That.

chef d'orchestre [F., shehf duhr-KEHSTR] Conductor.

chevalet [F., sheuh-va-LEH] Bridge of violins, etc. See *bowing (special effects)*.

cheville [F., sheuh-VEEY] Peg of stringed instruments.

chiaramente [It., kyah-rah-MEN-tay] Clearly, distinctly.

chiave [It., kee-AH-vay] Clef.

chiesa [It., kee-EH-sah] *da chiesa* – baroque term designating a piece for instruments, or voice with instruments, intended for use in the church.

chimes See *Percussion Instruments (6)*.

Chinese temple blocks A series of ornate wood blocks (usually five), roughly tuned to a pentatonic scale. Also called *temple blocks*.

chitarra [It., kee-TAHR-rah] Guitar.

choir 1. A group of singers in a church. 2. A group of similar instruments, e.g., brass choir; a group of strings on a harpsichord, comprising a *register*.

choir organ The third manual on an organ, useful for accompanying.

Chor [G., kohr] Chorus; choir.

choral Relating to a choir.

chorale; Choral [G., kohr-AHL] A hymn of the German Protestant Church. J.S. Bach composed numerous *chorales*. Following are various terms for organ works based on chorales: 1. chorale fantasia, 2. chorale fugue, 3. chorale prelude, 4. chorale variations (Choralpartita [G.]).

chorale cantata A cantata employing chorale texts and, usually, chorale melodies.

chord Three or more tones sounded together. Technically speaking, two simultaneous tones constitute a chord fragment. Also see *Table of Common Chords, inversion, sixth chord, seventh chord, triad*.

chordophones See *instruments*.

Chorlied [G., KOHR-leet] Choral song, usually sung *a cappella*.

chorus 1. A large group of singers who perform in concert or in an operatic context, as distinct from a *choir*, which sings sacred music exclusively. Also see *choir*. 2. Music written for a chorus. 3. Refrain of a song. 4. See *organ pipes*.

chorusing Combining two or more closely tuned sound sources to produce changes in timbre and amplitude. See *electronic music*.

chromatic Proceeding by half steps. Also see *chromaticism, chromatic scale*.

chromaticism The use of chromatic tones and chords in music.

chromatic scale A scale which contains all of the semitones in an octave:

church modes See *Gregorian chant (I & II)*.

ciaccona [It., chahk-KOH-nah] Chaconne.

cinelli [It., chee-NEL-lee] Cymbals.

cinq [F., seh(n)k]; **cinque** [It., CHEEN-kway] Five.

circle of fifths An arrangement of the 12 keys in fifths as shown below:

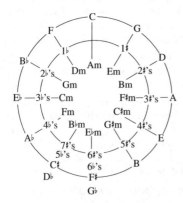

Cis [G., tsis] C sharp. See *pitch names*.

clarinet; clarinetto [It., klah-ree-NET-toh]; **clarinette** [F., kla-ree-NEHT] See *Woodwind Instruments (5)*.

clarinette basse [F., kla-ree-NEHT bas]; **clarinetto basso** [It., klah-ree-NET-toh BAHS-soh] Bass clarinet. See *Woodwind Instruments (6)*.

clarino Term applied to the high (valveless) trumpet and horn parts of the baroque period. 2. Italian term for *clarion*.

clarion 1. Medieval short trumpet favored by armies. Its high register led to the term *clarino*. 2. Organ stop like trumpet but of 4' pitch.

clarone [It., clah-ROH-nay] Bass clarinet.

classicism, classical period Terms denoting the Viennese classic school, i.e., Haydn, Mozart, Beethoven. See *History of Western Music*.

clavecin [F., klav-seh(n)] Harpsichord.

claves Cylindrical wood blocks which are struck together, used in Latin American music.

clavicembalo [It., klah-vee-CHEM-bah-loh] Harpsichord.

clavichord A keyboard instrument, a forerunner of the piano, in use from the 15th- through the 18th-centuries. Its strings are struck by *tangents* – small upright metal pins attached to the ends of the keys. The sound of the clavichord is soft but capable of subtle dynamic variations. Also see *Bebung*.

clavier [F., kla-VYAY]; **Klavier** [G., klah-VEER] 1. Keyboard. 2. A generic term, esp. from the baroque period, for the harpsichord, organ, and clavichord.

clef A sign at the beginning of a staff to indicate the pitch of the notes.

CLEFS CURRENTLY IN USE

Treble
(G clef)

Bass
(F clef)

C Clef
Indicates the position of Middle C
1. Soprano   2. Alto   3. Tenor

click track An automatic recording of beats, each one represented by a "click." Click tracks are useful during recording, since they keep perfect time. For instance, by using a click track live performance can be combined with computer-generated performance.

cloche [F., kluhsh] Bell. *cloches* – (F.) Bells, esp. orchestral bells.

cloches tubulaires [F., kluhsh tu(e)-bu(e)-LEHR] "Tubular bells." Chimes.

close Cadence.

close harmony Chords in *close position.*

close position The spacing of the notes in a chord so that the upper three notes are spaced together as closely as possible.

A) Close position

B) Open position

With *open position,* this restriction does not apply (Ex. B).

cluster See *tone cluster.*

coda [It., KOH-dah] Concluding section or passage. Also see *sonata form.*

codetta [It., koh-DET-tah] 1. A short coda. 2. A transitional section between two entries of the subject in a fugue.

col arco [It., kohl AHR-koh] With the bow (cancels *pizzicato*).

colla, coll' [It., KOHL-lah, kohl] "With the." *colla destra* – with the right hand; *colla sinistra* – with the left hand; *colla parte (voce)* – with the part or voice; *colla punta d'arco* – with the point of the bow.

col legno See *bowing (special effects).*

coll' ottava [It., kohl oht-TAH-vah] At the octave; duplicate the written notes an octave higher. *coll' ottava bassa* – duplicate notes an octave lower.

coloratura [It., koh-loh-rah-TOO-rah] In vocal music, a rapid virtuoso passage or embellishment, esp. in the *aria.*

combination tone, resultant tone An acoustic phenomenon where a tone of a different pitch is heard when two primary tones are sounded simultaneously. It may be either the sum or the difference of the two principal tones or of their multiples.

come [It., KOH-may] As, like. *come prima, come sopra* – as at first, as above; *come stà* – as it stands (without improvisation).

comic opera See *opera.*

comma 1. A minute difference in pitch occurring when intervals are calculated through different combinations of intervallic ratios. Commas are expressed in *cents.* 2. Breath mark (').

common chord Major triad.

common meter, time 4/4 meter.

Communion See *Mass.*

comodo [It., KOH-moh-doh] Comfortably, easily, without haste.

compass The range of an instrument.

composition 1. A musical work. 2. The process of creating a musical work.

compound interval Interval larger than an octave. See *interval*.

compound meter See *meter*.

compound stop Mixture stop of an organ.

con [It., kohn] With.

concertant [F., koh(n)-sehr-TAH(N)], **concertante** [It., kohn-chehr-TAHN-tay] An 18th-century name for a symphonic work employing one or more soloists; a successor to the *concerto grosso*.

concertina A small instrument of the accordion family.

concertino [It., kohn-cher-TEE-noh] 1. See *concerto grosso*. 2. A shorter, lighter type of *concerto*.

concertmaster The first violinist of an orchestra. The concertmaster usually plays the solo passages.

concerto [It., kohn-CHER-toh] Most commonly, a composition for a solo instrument and orchestra. The concerto usually has three movements; the first movement being a modified sonata form, the second a slow movement, and the third a lively, brilliant finale.

concerto grosso [It., kohn-CHER-toh GROHS-soh] Baroque form of the *concerto*. The full orchestra is called concerto (grosso) or *ripieno*; this group usually consists of a string orchestra. The soloists are called *concertino* or principale, usually consisting of two violins (and *basso continuo*). Early examples of the form contain suite-like movements; later, Vivaldi (1669-1741) used the scheme allegro-adagio-allegro.

concord, discord *Concord* – pleasant or consonant sounds; *discord* – unpleasant or dissonant sounds.

conga drum A long, narrow one-headed drum, used in Latin-American and popular music. Played with the hands.

conjunct, disjunct *Conjunct* – Proceeding by steps. Refers to melodic notes separated by a second. *Disjunct* – Proceeding by skips. Refers to melodic notes separated by a third or larger.

consecutive intervals Intervals of like size in immediate succession.

consequent See *antecedent*.

conservatory School specializing in music instruction and training.

console The case of an organ (including keyboard, stops, etc.) or electronic keyboard control panel.

consonance, dissonance Terms used to describe the aesthetic effect of intervals (and chords).

Prior to the 20th-century, consonant intervals were generally the octave, fifth, fourth, third, and sixth. Dissonant intervals were the major second, tritone, major seventh, etc. Historically, the concept of consonance and dissonance has undergone radical changes. The general trend, however, has been an increased tolerance of dissonance, esp. in the 20th-century.

con sordino [It., kohn sohr-DEE-noh] With mute.

consort 1. A 17th-century English term for an instrumental chamber ensemble. 2. A composition written for a consort.

contemporary music 1. The serious art music of our time. (The term "20th-century music" is no longer synonymous with contemporary music.) 2. Current popular music.

continuo See *thoroughbass*.

continuous controller See *electronic music*.

contra [It., KOHN-trah] "Against." As a prefix, it indicates a part which is an octave below, e.g., *contrabassoon*.

contrabass; contrabasso [It., kohn-trah-BAHS-soh] Double bass.

contrabassoon See *Woodwind Instruments (8)*.

contrafagotto [It., kohn-trah-fah-GOT-toh] Contrabassoon.

contralto See *voices, range of*.

contrappunto [It., kohn-trahp-POON-toh] *Counterpoint*.

contrapuntal In the style of *counterpoint*.

contrary motion See *motion*.

contrebasse [F., koh(n)-treuh-BAHS] Double bass.

contrebasson [F., koh(n)-treuh-bah-SOH(N)] Contrabassoon.

contredanse [F., koh(n)-treuh-DAH(N)S] An 18th-century dance performed by couples facing each other, accompanied by music consisting of repeated eight-measure phrases.

control processor A synthesizer function which is used to alter a control signal (voltage). Also see *electronic music*.

control voltage In electronic music, an electrical signal (voltage) used to control parameters such as pitch, timbre, and loudness. See *electronic music*.

controller A module which produces a *control voltage*. The synthesizer keyboard is an example of a controller. See *electronic music*.

coperto [It., koh-PEHR-toh] Covered. *timpani coperti* – timpani muted with a cloth.

copyright, musical Laws protecting printed and recorded works by composers and publishers. Copyrights govern reproduction, distribution, and public performance. Indicated by the symbol ©. More information can be obtained by writing the Copyright Office, The Library of Congress, Washington, DC 20540.

cor [F., kuhr] Horn (French horn).

cor anglais [F., kuhr ah(n)-GLEH] English horn.

coranto See *courante*.

corda [It., KOHR-dah], **corde** [F., kuhrd] "String." *una corda* – in piano music, the left (soft) pedal, canceled by *tre corde. corde à vide, corda vuota* – open violin string.

corista [It., koh-REES-tah] Orchestral pitch; tuning fork.

cornet; cornetta [It., kohr-NET-tah] Small brass instrument similar to the trumpet.

corno [It., KOHR-noh] Horn; French horn.

corno inglese [It., KOHR-noh een-GLAY-seh] English horn.

coro [It., KOH-roh] Choir; chorus.

corona [L., It., koh-ROH-nah] Pause, fermata ⌒

corrente [It., kohr-REN-tay] See *courante*.

cortège [F., kuhr-TEHZH] Composition written for a solemn procession, such as a funeral.

coulisse [F., koo-LEES] Trombone slide.

counter-fugue A fugue in which the first answer is an inversion of the subject. Example: Bach, *Art of Fugue, No. 5*.

counterpoint Music in which two or more independent lines sound simultaneously. Harmony is implied by 1) melody, and 2) the interaction of the voices.

countersubject See *fugue*.

country music Also known as country-western, or country and western. An American popular music style often characterized by simple narrative songs sung in cut time (¢), with guitar accompaniment.

While country music still evokes the image of the "singing cowboy" accompanying himself with a guitar, the reality is that country music is now as diverse and sophisticated as other popular idioms. Some important contributors to country music are: Hank Williams, George Jones, and Johnny Cash.

coup d'archet [F., koo dar-SHEH] Bow stroke.

coup de langue [F., koo deuh LAH(N)G] Tonguing.

coupler Mechanism which connects pedals with manuals, or different manuals of an organ or harpsichord together.

couplet [F., koo-PLEH] 1. Stanza of a poem. The music is repeated with each stanza. 2. The sections of the 17th-century rondeau, connected by a refrain. 3. A witty song in strophic form.

courante [F., koo-RAH(N)T]; **corrente** [It., kohr-REN-teh]; **coranto** A 16th-century dance form in triple meter, which became a standard movement of the suite. It is often characterized by *hemiola*. Also see *suite*.

course A set of unison strings, played simultaneously or consecutively for added volume.

cow bell, cowbell Similar to an actual cow bell, but without a clapper. Played with a drumstick.

crab canon A canon using the principle of retrograde. (See *retrograde*.)

crab motion See *retrograde*.

Credo [L., KREH-doh] See *Mass*.

crescendo [It., kray-SHEN-doh] Abbr. *cresc.* Indicated by ⟨ Becoming louder.

croche [F., kruhsh] Eighth note. (See *notes*.)

croisez, croisement [F., krwah-ZAY, krwahz-MAH(N) Cross the hands.

croma [It., KROH-mah] Eighth note. (See *notes*.)

cromorne [F., kroh-MUHRN] 1. Krummhorn. 2. A reed organ stop.

crook A short tube added to a horn to change its key.

cross-relation Displacement of a note in a progression to produce a "diagonal" resolution, considered bad in traditional counterpoint. The clash is more acceptable when the cross-relation occurs between middle voices, as shown here.

Normal resolution   Cross-relation

crotales [F., kro-TAL]; **crotali** [It., kroh-TAH-lee] See *Percussion Instruments (7)*.

crotchet (Brit.) Quarter note. (See *notes*.)

cue 1. A short passage taken from another part, inserted to aid the player. Cues are never played. 2. A signal for a performer to begin his/her musical passage.

cuivre [F., kweevr] Brass. (Literally, "copper.") *cuivré* – forced; harsh.

cycle 1. In acoustics, the unit of measure of a sound wave; one complete vibration of a sound source

Frequencies are measured in cycles per second., e.g., A440.

2. A composition in which the same thematic material is used in some or all of the movements.

cymbales antiques [F., seh(n)-BAL ah(n)-TEEK] Crotales. See *Percussion Instruments (7).*

cymbals; cymbales (F.) *See Percussion Instruments (13).*

D

D. See *pitch names*.

da capo [It., dah KAH-poh] From the beginning. Abbr. *D.C.*

da capo al segno – from the beginning to the sign 𝄋

da capo al fine – from the beginning to the *fine* (end).

daisy-chaining, daisy chaining Connecting sound modules via MIDI IN and MIDI THRU, allowing each to be operated by a single instrument (master keyboard). See *electronic music*.

dal segno [It., dahl SEH-nyoh] From the sign 𝄋. Abbr. *D.S.* (Return to the sign and repeat.) *dal segno al fine* – return to the sign and continue until the word *fine* (end).

damper In pianos and harpsichords, the part of the mechanism that stops the vibration of the string as the key is released.

damper pedal See *pedal*.

Dämpfer [G., DA(E)MP-fer] 1. See *damper*. 2. Mute.

decay Amplitude characteristics having to do with the ending of a sound or signal. *decay rate* – rate of change from peak level to sustain level within a sound envelope. Also see *envelope; electronic music*.

deceptive cadence See *cadence*.

decibel Abbr. *db*. Standard unit measuring loudness. Musical sounds range from about 25 db (*ppp*) to 100 db (*ff*).

deciso [It., deh-CHEE-zoh] Decided, definite.

decrescendo [It., deh-kreh-SHEN-doh] Abbr. *decresc, decr.* Indicated by

⟍⟍⟍ Becoming softer.

degrees Numbers assigned to the notes of a scale; e.g., C Major:

C	D	E	F	G	A	B
1	2	3	4	5	6	7

dehors, en [F., ah(n) deuh-UHR] Emphasized.

del, della [It., del, DEL-lah] Of the, by the.

demi- (F.) Half. *demi-pause* – half rest; *demi-soupir* – eighth rest. See *notes*.

demi-jeu [F., deuh-mee-ZHEUH] Half organ (softer registration).

demisemiquaver (Brit.) Thirty-second note. (See *notes*.)

derb [G., dehrb] Robust, rough.

Des [G., dehs] D flat. See *pitch names*.

descant A high obbligato part in hymn-singing.

desto [It., DES-toh] Briskly.

destra, destro [It., DES-trah, DES-troh] Right (hand).

détaché See *bowing (2)*.

detuning Slightly altering one of two otherwise identical pitches, or the timbral effect resulting from this interaction.

deutlich [G., DOYT-likh] Clear, distinct.

deux [F., deuh] Two.

development 1. The elaboration of musical material within a composition. 2. See *sonata form.*

Dezime [G., deh-TSEE-meh] Interval of the 10th.

di [It., dee] Of, with, for, from.

diapason The main foundation stop of the organ. (See *organ pipes.*)

diatonic Relating to a "white key" scale or its transposition; that is, a scale having no chromatic alterations. For instance, C D E F is diatonic; C D♯ E F is not.

diatonicism Music which is primarily diatonic.

dice music Same as *aleatory music.*

dieci [It., dee-EH-chee] Ten.

dièse [F., dee-EHZ] The sharp sign (♯).

digital See *analog; electronic music.*

digital music synthesis See *electronic music.*

diluendo [It., dee-loo-EN-doh] Fading away.

diminished interval An interval which is one half step smaller than a perfect or minor interval, e.g., C-G♭. (See *interval.*)

diminished seventh chord See *seventh chord (4).*

diminished triad See *triad.*

diminuendo [It., dee-mee-noo-EN-doh] Abbr. *dim.* Becoming softer.

diminution 1. A decrease in the duration of the notes of a phrase or melody. The notes are usually halved in value, but further diminution is possible.

A)

B) Diminution of A)

Also see *augmentation.*

2. A technique of ornamentation in which melody is broken up into quick figured passages.

DIN plug See *electronic music.*

dirge A song of grief; a composition for performance at a funeral or memorial service.

Dirigent [G., dir-i-GENT] Conductor.

dirigieren [G., dir-i-GEE-ren] To conduct.

Dis [G., dis] D sharp. See *pitch names.*

discant 1. A type of polyphonic music in which a melody is composed above a plainsong in the tenor. 2. The upper part of a polyphonic composition.

discord See *concord.*

disjunct See *conjunct.*

disposition The arrangement of stops, manuals, pedals, etc., of an organ or harpsichord.

dissonance See *consonance.*

divertimento [It., dee-vehr-tee-MEN-toh] A light instrumental composition, usually having several short movements.

divertissement [F., dee-vehr-tees-MAH(N)] See *divertimento.*

divisi [It., dee-VEE-see] Abbr. *div.* Indication for players reading on one staff to divide into two or more groups.

dix [F., dees] Ten.

do See *pitch names, solmization.*

dodecaphonic See *serial music.*

dodecuple scale Twelve-tone scale. (Also see *serial music.*)

dodici [It., DOH-dee-chee] Twelve.

doigté [F., dwah-TAY] Fingering.

dolce [It., DOHL-chay] Sweetly.

dolcissimo [It., dohl-CHEES-see-moh] Very sweetly.

dolente, doloroso [It., doh-LEN-tay, doh-loh-ROH-soh] Sorrowful.

dominant The fifth degree of a scale. (See *scale degrees*.) 2. See *Gregorian chant*. *dominant triad* – The triad based on the fifth degree of a scale, represented by the numeral V.

dominant seventh chord See *seventh chord (1)*.

Donner [G., DON-ner] Thunder.

dopo [It., DOH-poh] After.

doppel [G., DOH-pel] Double.

doppelt so schnell [G., DOH-pelt zoh shnell] Twice as fast.

doppio [It., DOHP-pyoh] Double. *doppio movimento* – Twice as fast.

Dorian mode See *Gregorian chant III*.

dot 1. A dot placed after a note increases its duration by 1/2:

$$ \text{♩.} = \text{♩} + \text{♪} $$

Two dots increase its duration by 1/2 plus 1/4: $\text{♩..} = \text{♩} + \text{♪} + \text{♪}$

2. A dot above or below a note indicates *staccato*. Also see *bowing*.

double A type of baroque variation, usually with melodic diminutions and embellishments.

double bar See *bar*.

double bass See *Violin Family (4)*.

double bassoon Contrabassoon.

double chorus The use of two choruses in alternation.

double concerto A concerto for two solo instruments and orchestra.

double corde [F., doobl kuhrd] Double stop.

double counterpoint See *invertible counterpoint*.

double-croche [F., doobl-kruhsh] Sixteenth note. (See *notes*.)

double flat ♭♭ Lowers a tone by two half steps.

double fugue A fugue with two subjects. Also see *fugue*.

double note Same as *breve*.

double octave The interval of two octaves, i.e., the 15th.

double reed See *reed*.

double sharp 𝄪 Raises a tone by two half steps.

double stop For instruments of the violin family: Two tones played at the same time.

double tonguing See *tonguing*.

doubly-augmented fourth chord See *sixth chords*.

doucement [F., doos-MAH(N)] Gently, tenderly.

douloureux [F., doo-loo-REUH] Sorrowful.

doux [F., doo] Sweet, soft, gentle.

douze [F., dooz] Twelve.

down-bow The downward stroke of the bow in violin playing. (See *bowing [1]*.) Occasionally spelled *downbow*, *down bow*, although these spellings are not recommended.

downbeat Downward motion of the conductor's hand; first beat of a measure.

doxology An expression of praise sung after a psalm, canticle, prayer, or hymn.

drei [G., drei] Three.

dreifach [G., DREI-fakh] Triple.

Dreiklang [G., DREI-klahng] Triad.

dritte [G., DRI-teh] Third.

drone 1. See *bagpipe*. 2. Long, sustained (low) notes which support melodic or chordal passages.

drum A percussion instrument consisting of a resonant hollow cylinder with a *head* at one or both ends. (The head is a thin membrane of skin or plastic.) Played with the hands or with sticks. Also see *Percussion Instruments*.

drum set, drum kit The drum set used by rock and jazz drummers consists of the following: ride and crash cymbals; hi-hat (two small cymbals on a  stand which are clicked together by a foot pedal); snare drum; a small bass drum played by a foot pedal; tom-toms (high-pitched drums, often paired); and a "floor tom," a large tom-tom with a low tone.

due [It., DOO-ay] Two.

due corde [It., doo-ay KOHR-day] "Two strings." In violin music, an indication to play the same tone on two strings.

duet A composition for two performers.

due volte [It., doo-ay VOHL-tay] Twice.

dulciana An 8-foot organ string stop with a thin and mild tone.

dulcimer 1. A stringed instrument with a flat, usually trapezoidal, soundboard. It is played by striking the strings with small hammers, hence the term "hammer dulcimer." 2. In Appalachian music, the dulcimer is a 3-stringed instrument with a fretted fingerboard played with the fingers.

dumka [Russ., DOOM-kah] 1. Ukrainian folk ballad. 2. A type of instrumental music that contains sudden changes of mood.

duo Duet.

Duodezime [G., doo-oh-deh-TSEE-meh]; **duodecima** [It., doo-oh-DEH-chee-mah] Interval of the 12th.

Duole [G., doo-OH-leh]; **duolet** [F., du(e)-oh-LEH] Duplet.

duple meter See *meter*.

duplet A group of two notes played in the time of three.

Dur [G., doohr] Major.

duramente [It., doo-rah-MEN-tay] Harshly.

duration The length of time a tone is held.

dynamics 1. Degrees of softness and loudness. 2. Symbols or words which indicate degrees of softness or loudness, e.g.,

E

E. See *pitch names*.

Ecclesiastical modes See *Gregorian chant (II – church modes)*.

échappée See *nonharmonic tones I (4)*.

échelette [F., ay-sheuh-LEHT] Xylophone.

échelle [F., ay-SHEHL] Scale.

echo; eco [It., EH-koh] 1. Acoustics: Audible reiteration of a sound at a lower volume. 2. Repetition or imitation of a motif or passage, at a lower volume.

écossaise [F., ay-kuh-SEHZ] A country dance in quick 2/4 meter.

eguale [It., eh-GWAH-lay] Equal; alike.

eighth An octave.

eighth note, rest See *notes*.

eilen [G., EI-len] To hasten, to accelerate. *eilend, eilig* – rapid, swift. *mit Eile* – hurrying.

ein, eins, eine(n) [G., ein(s), EIN-en] A; one.

einfach [G., EIN-fakh] Simple.

Eingang [G., EIN-gahng] Entrance, introduction. A "lead-in," usually improvised, between sections.

Einhalt [G., EIN-hahlt] A pause, interruption.

Einklang [G., EIN-klahng] Unison.

Einleitung [G., EIN-lei-toong] Introduction.

Einsatz [G., EIN-zahts] 1. Attack. 2. Entrance of a part. 3. Cue.

Eis [G., eis] E sharp. See *pitch names*.

Eintritt [G., EIN-tritt] Entrance, esp. a fugal subject.

electric bass See *bass guitar*.

ELECTRONIC MUSIC

Music which is produced by purely electronic means, such as a sound synthesizer. Electronic music differs from *musique concrète*, which is made by altering and/or combining recorded sounds.

How electronic music is made

The basic sound-producing device used to create electronic sounds is the *oscillator*. Oscillators produce simple waveforms, which are then filtered and passed through an envelope generator:

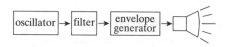

Oscillator. An *oscillator* can produce one of the following wave types:

1. Sine
2. Sawtooth
3. Triangle
4. Square

Filter. A sound wave is sent through a *filter*, a device which allows selected frequencies to pass through while suppressing others. Below are the basic types of filters:

1. High pass filter –

    allows only frequencies *above* a cut-off frequency to pass (sound).

2. Low pass filter –

    allows only frequencies *below* a cut-off frequency to pass (sound).

3. Band pass filter –

    allows only a specific band of frequencies to pass.

4. Band reject filter –

    eliminates a specific band of frequencies and allows all others to pass.

Envelope generator. The *envelope generator* shapes the amplitude characteristics of a sound. The amplitude characteristics of a sound are referred to as an *envelope*. The envelope generator is divided into four settings, which can be adjusted individually:

1. attack   3. sustain

2. decay   4. release

These settings are abbreviated as ADSR.

Audio out. The sound is amplified and broadcast over speakers.

Analog Music Synthesis

Analog music synthesis (which predates MIDI technology) began to be exploited by composers such as Stockhausen and Xenakis during the 1950s. Using simple oscillators, filters, etc., composers laboriously created complex sounds "from scratch," i.e., from simple waveforms. Compositions were assembled gradually onto magnetic tape, without the aid of computers.

The most important analog technique of creating complex waveforms is that of *control voltage*. Here voltages are used to control basic qualities (parameters) such as pitch, timbre, and loudness. (The use of voltage to control sound differs from digital synthesis, where MIDI code is used to control and represent sound information. See *Digital Music Synthesis*, later in this essay.)

Below are two common analog processes utilizing control voltages:

amplitude modulation (AM) – A periodic fluctuation in loudness. AM is produced by connecting an oscillator (OSC) to a *voltage-controlled amplifier* (VCA); the amplitude of the VCA is affected by another voltage source. Tremolo is an example of amplitude modulation.

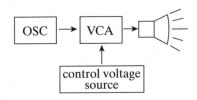

frequency modulation (FM) – A periodic fluctuation in pitch. FM is produced by a *voltage-controlled oscillator* (VCO); the pitch of the VCO is affected by another voltage source. Vibrato is an example of frequency modulation.

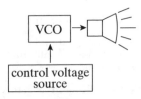

Two sound sources can also modulate each other. The following are common examples:

ring modulation – Two sound sources modulating each other, producing the sums and differences of the two while eliminating the originals. Ring-modulated sounds are "metallic" in quality.

chorusing – Combining two or more closely tuned sound sources to produce changes in timbre and amplitude.

Digital Music Synthesis

Digital music synthesis has been around since the advent of the compact disc (ca.1980). Any kind of sound – acoustic or electronic – can now be converted into digital information.

A *sampler* is a synthesizer which can record a sound digitally. After a sound has been sampled, it can be played on any key of a synthesizer. Its pitch rises or falls depending upon which key is struck. Sampled sounds can also be stored as preset sounds in modules, enabling composers and performers to mimic the sounds of all available acoustic instruments.

Of course, any digitally-recorded sound can be altered or transformed into totally new sounds.

MIDI

In digital music synthesis, *MIDI* data is used to control sound parameters. A brief description of MIDI follows:

MIDI – Definition: Acronym for Musical Instrument Digital Interface, a type of digital code which allows synthesizers and computers to communicate with each other.

Midi Connectors (ports)

MIDI uses *serial transmission*: data travels one bit at a time in a one-way stream. Since the same port cannot be used for both sending and receiving MIDI data, three different connectors are used:

MIDI In   – receives MIDI data
MIDI Out – sends MIDI data
MIDI Thru – reroutes MIDI IN data

(MIDI connectors use a 5-pin plug called a *DIN plug*.)

MIDI THRU

MIDI Thru is useful for "daisy-chaining" sound modules, allowing each to be operated by a single instrument.

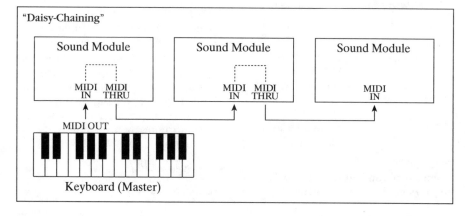

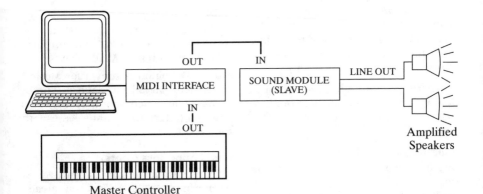

Master Controller

SIMPLE SEQUENCER SETUP
(Computer and keyboard)

Above is a typical setup involving a keyboard (controller), a computer (or sequencer), a sound module, and speakers.

Note: In order to connect a computer with a synthesizer, a MIDI interface is required. A MIDI interface is a cabling device equipped with MIDI In and MIDI Out connectors.

Keyboard (controller)

In addition to keys, the master keyboard houses *continuous controllers*, used to effect expressive changes. Some common types of continuous controllers are:

sustain pedal – "damper" pedal

pitch bend wheel – produces pitch bends

modulation wheel – produces vibrato effects

aftertouch – pressure applied to a key after it is struck, which sends additional MIDI data

Sequencer

Computers run sequencer software. A *sequencer* is a sort of MIDI "tape re-corder," without tape. Instead of tape, MIDI data is used to record and play back instrumental performances.

A complete performance is called a *sequence*. It is stored as a MIDI file – a computer file containing all of the MIDI data needed to execute the performance. MIDI files are standard in format and can be moved from one computer sequencer to another (such as from Performer to Finale).

The sequencer divides music into *channels* – pathways used to transmit and receive MIDI data. To avoid duplication, each "instrument" is assigned its own channel. A single MIDI cable can handle up to 16 channels.

Editing with a sequencer

Since music is stored as MIDI data, it can be edited within the sequencer software.

Some MIDI data can be edited by the sequencer itself. *Quantization*, for instance, is a process where rhythms are rounded off to a predesignated rhythmic value. For example, if the value chosen is an eighth note, then no values smaller than eighth notes will be allowed.

Ex. played: ♪♪♪ ♩♪

quantized: ♫ ♫

Quantization routines are especially useful in simplifying overly-accurate transcriptions of human performance, as in the preceding example.

Other editing features are initiated by the user, such as: 1) transposition, 2) dynamic and attack alterations, 3) ability to cut and paste selected music.

Sound Module

A sound module contains a variety of preset sounds. Each sound is called a *program*, or *patch*. A specific number is assigned by the manufacturer to each program, e.g. 33 = acoustic bass, 109 = kalimba. (When a different program is invoked by a sequencer, it is called a *program change*.)

Some sound modules are capable of producing only one program at a time. Normally modules of this kind are assigned a single MIDI channel. A *multi-timbral module* is capable of playing several programs at once. Several channels can be routed to a single multi-timbral module to produce an ensemble effect.

Most non-specialized multi-timbral sound modules subscribe to the General MIDI format. General MIDI is a standardized set of sounds; the assigned numbers are the same for all manufacturers. (For example, 72 always equals clarinet.)

Below is the General MIDI sound list:

1	acoustic grand piano	30	overdrive guitar	65	soprano sax	99	FX 3 (crystal)
2	bright acoustic piano	31	distortion guitar	66	alto sax	100	FX 4 (atmosphere)
3	electric grand piano	32	guitar harmonics	67	tenor sax	101	FX 5 (brightness)
4	honky-tonk piano	33	acoustic bass	68	baritone sax	102	FX 6 (goblins)
5	electric piano 1	34	electric bass (finger)	69	oboe	103	FX 7 (echoes)
6	electric piano 2	35	electric bass (pick)	70	English horn	104	FX 8 (sci-fi)
7	harpischord	36	fretless bass	71	bassoon	105	sitar
8	clavi	37	slap bass 1	72	clarinet	106	banjo
9	celesta	38	slap bass 2	73	piccolo	107	shamisen
10	glockenspiel	39	synth bass 1	74	flute	108	koto
11	music box	40	synth bass 2	75	recorder	109	kalimba
12	vibraphone	41	violin	76	pan flute	110	bagpipe
13	marimba	42	viola	77	blown bottle	111	fiddle
14	xylophone	43	cello	78	shakuhachi	112	shanai
15	tubular bells	44	contrabass	79	whistle	113	tinkle bell
16	dulcimer	45	tremolo strings	80	ocarina	114	agogo
17	drawbar organ	46	pizzicato strings	81	lead 1 (square)	115	steel drums
18	percussive organ	47	orchestral harp	82	lead 2 (sawtooth)	116	wood block
19	rock organ	48	timpani	83	lead 3 (calliope)	117	taiko drum
20	church organ	49	string ensemble 1	84	lead 4 (chiff)	118	melodic tom
21	reed organ	50	string ensemble 2	85	lead 5 (charang)	119	synth drum
22	accordion	51	synth strings 1	86	lead 6 (voice)	120	reverse cymbal
23	harmonica	52	synth strings 2	87	lead 7 (fifths)	121	guitar fret noise
24	bandoneon	53	choir aahs	88	lead 8 (bass + lead)	122	breath noise
25	guitar (nylon)	54	voice oohs	89	pad 1 (new age)	123	seashore
26	acoustic guitar (steel)	55	synth voice	90	pad 2 (warm)	124	bird tweet
27	electric guitar (jazz)	56	orchestra hit	91	pad 3 (polysynth)	125	telephone ring
28	electric guitar (clean)	57	trumpet	92	pad 4 (choir)	126	helicopter
29	electric guitar (muted)	58	trombone	93	pad 5 (bowed glass)	127	applause
		59	tuba	94	pad 6 (metallic)	128	gunshot
		60	muted trumpet	95	pad 7 (halo)		
		61	French horn	96	pad 8 (sweep)		
		62	brass section	97	FX 1 (rain)		
		63	synth brass 1	98	FX 2 (soundtrack)		
		64	synth brass 2				

eleganza [It., eh-leh-GAHN-tsah] Elegance, grace.

elegia [It., eh-leh-JEE-ah]; **elegy** A mournful composition.

elf [G., elf] Eleven.

embellishment Ornament.

embouchure (F.) 1. In wind playing, proper position of the lips. 2. Mouthpiece of a wind instrument.

Empfindung, mit [G., mit emp-FIN-doong] With feeling.

empressé [F., ah(n)-preh-SAY Eager, pressing.

ému [F., ay-MU(E)] With emotion; moved, touched.

en [F., ah(n)] In.

enchaînez [F., ah(n)-sheh-NAY] Chain together; join two sections without a break (*attacca*).

encore A short piece played at the conclusion of a concert in response to enthusiastic applause.

energico [It., en-EHR-jee-koh] With energy, vigor.

English horn; englisches Horn [G., EN-glish-es hohrn] See *Woodwind Instruments (4)*.

enharmonic Refers to tones of the same pitch but which are spelled differently, e.g., C♯-D♭, A♭-G♯.

ensemble Musical group, often *ad hoc* rather than a standard group such as a string quartet; e.g., a modern music ensemble.

entr'acte [F., ah(n)-TRAKT] A piece of music performed between two acts of a play or opera.

entschieden, entschlossen [G., ent-SHEE-den, ent-SHLOH-sen] Determined, resolute.

envelope Amplitude characteristics which determine the growth and decay of a signal; i.e.,A) attack, B) decay, C) sustain, D) release. Also see *electronic music*.

envelope follower In electronic music, a device which converts pitch to a control voltage. In a typical setup, an instrument plays into a microphone; the envelope follower converts the audio output into *control voltages* to control a *voltage controlled amplifier*.

envelope generator A module of the music synthesizer which allows the elements of an *envelope* to be controlled individually, such as loudness and timbre. There are adjustable settings for attack, decay, sustain, and release times (ADSR).

With respect to digital sampling synthesizers, envelope characteristics are inherent in the sampled sounds. Usually envelopes are edited by means of sound editing computer software. See *electronic music*.

épinette [F., ay-pee-NEHT] Spinet, virginal, harpsichord.

episode See *fugue*.

equalizer An electronic device for increasing or decreasing the signal strength of discrete frequency bands. This device changes the "color" (harmonic content) of a sound.

equal temperament A system of tuning in which the octave is divided into 12 equal semitones. Equal temperament is the system currently in use. Also see *just intonation*; *Pythagorean scale*.

erlöschend [G., ehr-LO(E)-shent] Fading away.

ermattend [G., ehr-MAH-tent] Tiring, weakening.

ernst, ernsthaft [G., ehrnst, EHRNST-hahft] Serious(ly).

eroico [It., eh-ROY-koh] "Heroic."

erst [G., ehrst] First.

escape tone Same as *échappée*.

Es [G., es] E flat. See *pitch names*.

esercizio [It., ez-ehr-CHEE-zee-oh] Exercise, etude.

espagnol [F., ehs-pa-NYUHL] Spanish.

espressione, con [It., kohn es-prehs-zee-OH-nay] With expression.

espressivo [It., es-pres-SEE-voh] Expressively.

estinto [It., eh-STEEN-toh], **éteint** [F., ay-TEH(N)] Dying away, barely audible.

et [F., ay] And.

ethnomusicology The study of music that is outside the European art music tradition, esp. in a cultural or sociological context.

étouffé [F., ay-too-FAY] Damped, muted.

étude A study, usually focusing on a single technical problem.

euphonium Brass instrument similar to the baritone, but with a larger bore.

exposition 1. See *sonata form*. 2. See *fugue*.

expression The emotional quality of music, as distinct from its intellectual quality. These emotional qualities cannot be notated; rather, it is the job of the interpreter to realize them in performance.

expressionism A style of early 20th-century German music which is both subjective and introspective. Schoenberg, Webern, and Berg are usually referred to as *expressionists*.

expressivo Incorrect spelling of *espressivo*.

F

F. 1. See *pitch names*. 2. Abbr. for *forte* (*f*)

fa See *pitch names*; *solmization*.

facile [F., fa-SEEL] [It., FAH-chee-lay] Easy, simple, facile.

Fagott [G., fah-GOT], **fagotto** [It., fah-GOT-toh] Bassoon.

falsetto Artificially high tones of the male voice.

fancy Obsolete term for *fantasy*; a term in use in England during the 16th and 17th-centuries for contrapuntal instrumental music in an imaginative style.

fandango [Sp., fahn-DAHN-goh] Lively Spanish dance in 3/4 time, traditionally accompanied by guitar and castanets.

fanfare Trumpet call, originally for valveless horns – hence, usually triadic.

fantasia [It., fahn-tah-SEE-yah], **Fantasie** [G., fahn-tah-SEE], **fantaisie** [F., fah(n)-teh-ZEE] Composition in an improvisational or dreamy style.

fantastico [It., fahn-TAHS-tee-koh], **fantastique** [F., fah(n)-tas-TEEK] Fantastic, grotesque.

fantasy See *fantasia*.

fastoso [It., fahs-TOH-soh] Pompous.

fauxbourdon [F., foh-boor-DOH(N)] Modern usage: Harmonic progression of parallel sixth chords.

F clef Bass clef. See *clef*.

feedback The return of the output of an amplifier to its input, which can result in an uncontrollable increase in volume. In electronic music, feedback is used under controlled circumstances, such as compositions involving tape loops.

feierlich [G., FEI-er-likh] Festive, solemn.

fermata [It., fehr-MAH-tah], **Fermate** [G., fehr-MAH-teh] A lengthening of a note or rest, indicated by the sign ⌢ Also called *pause*.

Ferne, aus der [G., aus dehr FEHR-neh] From the distance.

feroce [It., feh-ROH-chay] Wild, fierce.

fervente, con fervore [It., fehr-VEN-tay, kohn fehr-VOH-ray] Fervent, passionately.

Fes [G., fehs] F flat. See *pitch names*.

festivo, festoso [It., fes-TEE-voh, fes-TOH-soh] Festive, joyous.

fiato [It., FYAH-toh] Breath.

fiddle 1. Generic term for any stringed instrument played with a bow; but usually, the violin. 2. Medieval ancestor of the violin. 3. Folk violin.

fife; fifre [F., feefr] A small, shrill flute used in military bands, e.g., fife and drum corps.

fifteenth 1. Double octave. 2. Two-foot organ stop, sounding two octaves above normal.

fifth See *interval*.

figured bass See *thoroughbass*.

filter An electronic device which allows selected frequencies to pass through while suppressing others. See *electronic music*.

fin [F., feh(n)] End.

final, finalis See *Gregorian chant.*

finale [It., fee-NAH-lay] 1. The last movement of a sonata, symphony, etc. 2. The last piece of an operatic act.

fin' al segno [It., feen ahl SAY-nyoh] End at the sign ⅹ

fine [It., FEE-nay] End.

fingerboard The wooden surface below the strings of a violin, guitar, etc.

finger cymbals Crotales. See *percussion instruments (7).*

fingering A system of, or directions for, using the fingers when playing an instrument. Numbers are assigned to the fingers of each hand.

fioritura [It., fyohr-ee-TOO-rah] Embellishment.

first inversion See *inversion.*

Fis [G., fis] F sharp. See *pitch names.*

Fistelstimme [G., FIS-tel-shtim-meh] Falsetto.

fixed do See *solmization.*

flag See *notes.*

flageolet [F., fla-zhoh-LEH] 1. A recorder with four front holes and two thumb holes. 2. A 2-foot organ stop.

flageolet tones Harmonics. See *harmonic (2).*

flam A drumbeat of two strokes, the first being a quick grace note

flamenco (Sp., flah-MEN-koh] A vigorous, rhythmic dance style of Spanish (Andalusian) gypsies.

flat ♭ Lowers the pitch of a note by one half step.

flautando, flautato [It., flau-TAHN-doh, flau-TAH-toh] See *bowing (special effects).*

flauto [It., FLAU-toh] Flute. Before ca. 1850, *flauto* meant *recorder.*

flauto piccolo [It., FLAU-toh PEEK-koh-loh] Piccolo.

fliessend [G., FLEE-sent] Flowing.

florid Ornamented, embellished.

Flöte [G., FLO(E)-teh] Flute.

flourish 1. Brass fanfare. 2. A showy passage.

flue pipes See *organ pipes.*

Flügel [G., FLU(E)-gel] The grand piano.

flügelhorn; Flügelhorn [G., FLU(E)-gel-hohrn] A brass instrument similar to the cornet, but with a wider bore. Tuned in B♭. The flügelhorn is a common  substitute for the trumpet when a more mellow tone is desired.

flüssig [G., FLU(E)-sikh] Flowing.

flute; flûte [F., flu(e)t] See *Woodwind Instruments (2).*

fois [F., fwah] Time.

folk song 1. A song which reflects the life of a community or region. Folk songs are usually part of an oral tradition, so their origin cannot be traced to a single composer or author. In fact, often there are many versions of the same song.

2. A style of popular song which features simple melody and harmony, usually with acoustic guitar accompaniment. Its form is typically verse alternating with chorus; lyrics are usually narrative.

foot Unit of measure in organ pipes. When a key is depressed:

4 foot = 1 octave higher
8 foot = natural pitch
16 foot = octave lower

Mutation pipes are expressed in fractions, such as:

5-1/3 = perfect fifth higher

2-2/3 = 12th (octave + 5th) higher

form The structural outline of a composition, e.g., binary form, sonata form, etc.

fort [F., fuhr] Strong, loud.

forte [It., FOHR-tay] Abbr. *f.* Loud.

forte-piano [It., fohr-tay-pee-AH-noh] Abbr. *fp* Loud, followed immediately by soft.

fortepiano 1. Obsolete term for the piano. 2. Immediate predecessor of the piano, capable of producing dynamic contrasts. Its tone has considerable variety but is not as powerful as that of the modern piano.

fortissimo [It., fohr-TEES-see-moh] Abbr. *ff* Very loud.

fortississimo [It., fohr-tees-SEES-see-moh] Abbr. *fff* Very, very loud.

forza, con [It., kohn FOHR-sah] With force.

forzando, forzato [It., fohr-SAHN-doh, fohr-SAH-toh] Forced, accented.

foundation stops The unison and octave ranks of the organ (16', 8', 4'), esp. those of the principal chorus, but including flutes and strings also.

fourth See *interval.*

fourth chord A chord built of fourths, e.g., E-A-D, C-F-B♭.

Frauenchor [G., FRAU-en-kohr] Women's chorus.

frei [G., frei] Free, freely.

French horn See *horn.*

French sixth chord See *sixth chord.*

frequency The rate of vibration of a sound, measured in cycles per second (hertz). Frequency is the scientific measurement of *pitch.*

frequency modulation In electronic music, a periodic fluctuation of pitch (Abbr. FM). See *electronic music.*

frets Narrow strips placed across the fingerboard of guitars and other stringed instruments, in order to mark the positions for stopping the strings.

frisch [G., frish] Fresh, lively.

frog Part of a violin bow, near the grip. Also called *nut.*

fröhlich [G., FRO(E)-likh] Joyful.

F-Schlüssel [G., EF-shlu(e)-sel] Bass clef (F clef).

fuga [L., It., FOO-gah], **Fuge** [G., FOO-geh] Fugue. See *fugue.*

fugal imitation See *imitation; fugue.*

fugato [It., foo-GAH-toh] A passage or work in fugal style.

fugue A contrapuntal form, characterized by the following: At the beginning, a short theme or *subject* is announced alone by one voice. Then a second voice enters and announces the subject in the dominant – this announcement is called the *answer.* If the answer imitates the subject exactly at the perfect 5th, it is called *real;* otherwise, it is called *tonal.*

During an answer, the voice which announced the subject continues freely. If that continuation is of a consistent, thematic character, it is called a *countersubject.* A section in which the theme appears at least once in each voice is called the *exposition.* A fugal section with no statement of the subject is called an *episode.* (Episodes typically use short motifs taken from the subject or countersubject.)

After the episode, there are no strict procedures. Modulation is common, and there is a return to the tonic near the end. Often a *stretto* occurs at the close. A *stretto* is the imitation of a subject before it has been completely announced, producing an increase in intensity.

fundamental 1. Root of a chord. 2. See *harmonic*.

funebre [It., FOO-neh-breh], **funèbre** [F., fu(e)-NEHBR] Funereal, mournful.

funerale [It., foo-neh-RAH-lay] Funeral.

fünf [G., fu(e)nf] Five.

fuoco, con [It., kohn foo-OH-koh] With fire.

für [G., fu(e)r] For.

furioso [It., foo-ree-OH-soh] Furiously.

furore [It., foo-ROH-ray] Fury, rage.

G

G. See *pitch names.*

gai [F., gay] Gay, lively, brisk.

gain A quantity expressing the degree of amplification of an amplifier.

galant style The "elegant" style of the *rococo* (18th century), as distinct from the baroque.

galliard A lively 16th-century dance, with five steps in a measure ("cinq pas").

galop A lively 19th-century round dance in 2/4 meter, with a hopping rhythm.

gamba See *organ pipes.*

gamelan The orchestra of Bali and Java, usually consisting of drums, gongs, wooden flutes, and various metallophones (bronze-keyed xylophones).

gamma [It., GAHM-mah], **gamme** [F., gam] Scale.

ganz [G., gahnts] Whole, entire. *ganze Note* – whole note; *ganze Pause* – whole rest. See *notes.*

garbato, con garbo [It., gahr-BAH-toh, kohn GAHR-boh] Graceful, elegant.

gate With respect to electronic instruments: a control signal in effect while a key is being depressed.

gauche [F., gohsh] Left.

gavotte A 17th-century French dance, typically in moderate 2/2 meter, characterized by 1) an upbeat of two quarter notes, and 2) phrases which begin and end in the middle of the measure.

Gebrauchsmusik [G., geh-BRAUKHS-moo-zik] "Music for use." Music written for amateurs, or for informal use.

gebunden [G., geh-BOON-den] Tied; *legato.*

G clef See *clef.*

gedackt, gedeckt [G., geh-DAHKT, geh-DEHKT] Stopped.

gedämpft [G., geh-DA(E)MPFT] Muted, muffled.

gedehnt [G., geh-DAYNT] Lengthened, slow.

Gefühl [G., geh-FU(E)L] Feeling, expression.

gehalten [G., geh-HAHL-ten] Held out, sustained.

gehend [G., GAY-ent] Moving.

Geige [G., GEI-geh] Violin.

geistlich [G., GEIST-likh] Sacred, spiritual.

gelassen [G., geh-LAH-sen] Calm, quiet.

geläufig [G., geh-LOY-fikh] Fluent, easy.

gemächlich [G., geh-MA(E)KH-likh] Comfortable, easy-going.

gemässigt [G., geh-MA(E)-sikt] Moderate.

gemischt [G., geh-MISHT] Mixed. Organ: mixed stops.

gemütlich [G., geh-MU(E)T-likh] Cheerful, pleasant.

Generalbass [G., geh-na-RAHL-bahs] Same as *thoroughbass.*

general pause; Generalpause [G., geh-na-RAHL-pau-zeh] A rest for the entire ensemble. Abbr. G.P.

gentile [It., jen-TEE-lay] Graceful, amiable.

German flute An 18th-century name for the transverse (modern) flute.

German sixth chord See *sixth chord*.

Ges [G., gehs] G flat. See *pitch names*.

Gesang [G., geh-ZAHNG] Song. *gesangvoll – cantabile*.

geschleift [G., geh-SHLEIFT] Slurred, legato.

geschwind [G., geh-SHVINT] Quickly, nimbly.

gesteigert [G., geh-SHTEI-gehrt] Increased.

gestopft [G., geh-SHTOHPFT] Stopped notes on the horn.

gestossen [G., geh-SHTOH-sen] Separated, detached.

geteilt [G., geh-TEILT] Divided, *divisi*.

getragen [G., geh-TRAH-gen] Sustained, slow.

gigelira [It., jee-geh-LEE-rah] Xylophone.

gigue [F., zheeg], **giga** [It., JEE-gah] "Jig." A dance in 6/8 or 6/4 meter, usually the final movement of the suite. Also see *suite*.

giocondo [It., joh-KOHN-doh] Cheerful, merry.

giocoso [It., joh-KOH-soh] Humorous, playful.

gioioso, giojoso [It., joh-YOH-soh] Joyous, cheerful.

gioviale [It., joh-vee-AH-lay] Jovial.

giro [It., JEE-roh] Turn.

Gis [G., gis] G sharp. See *pitch names*.

gitana, alla [It., AHL-lah jee-TAH-nah] Gypsy style.

giubiloso [It., joo-bee-LOH-soh] Jubilant.

giustamente, giusto [It., joos-tah-MEN-tay, JOOS-toh] Just, right, exact. *tempo giusto* – strict tempo.

giustezza [It., joos-TET-tsah] Precision.

glass harmonica A series of tuned glasses, played by rubbing the fingers against the (wet) glass.

glee A type of 18th-century homophonic choral music for unaccompanied voices, usually male.

gleichmässig [G., GLEIKH-ma(e)-sikh] Even, regular.

glide *Portamento*.

glissando [It., glees-SAHN-doh], **gleiten** [G., GLEI-ten] A rapid gliding or sliding movement, such as sliding a finger nail over the white keys of the piano.

Glocke [G., GLOH-keh] Bell. *Glocken* – bells, chimes.

glockenspiel; Glockenspiel [G., GLOH-ken-shpeel] See *Percussion Instruments (2)*.

Gloria See *Mass*.

Gondellied [G., GON-dehl-leet], **gondoliera** [It., gon-doh-lee-AY-rah] Boat song.

gong See *Percussion Instruments (14)*.

gospel music A type of religious music originating in African-American Protestant churches; it is often fervent and rhythmic. As part of a church service, the music may involve a "call and response" between the preacher and the choir. It may also feature a soloist who vocalizes above the rhythmic accompaniment of the choir and organist (or pianist).

White gospel music is similar to black gospel with respect to its use in church services. Both black and white gospel styles have influenced popular music idioms. Also see *soul music.*

grace note A small ornamental note or notes placed before a principal note. It is usually played immediately before the beat, but in some instances it may be played at the same time as the principal note, and then immediately released.

gracieux [F., gra-SYEUH] Graceful.

gradamente [It., grah-dah-MEN-tay] Gradually.

Gradual See *Mass.*

gran [It., grahn] Great, grand, largo.

gran cassa, gran tamburo [It., grahn KAHS-sah, grahn tahm-BOO-roh] Bass drum.

grand [F., grah(n)] Great, grand.

grandezza, con [It., kohn grahn-DET-tsah] With grandeur.

grand jeu, grand orgue [F., grah(n) zheuh, grah(n) TUHRG] Full organ.

grand opera A serious opera of the 19th-century, sung throughout (no spoken dialogue). Also see *opera.*

grand pause See *general pause.*

grave [It., GRAH-vay] Grave, solemn.

gravità [It., grah-vee-TAH] Gravity, dignity.

grazia, grazioso [It., GRAH-tsee-ah, grah-tsee-OH-soh] Grace, gracefully.

great The manual of an organ controlling the *great organ.*

great organ Ranks of pipes containing the largest and most important stops of the organ.

GREGORIAN CHANT

I. The liturgical chant used in the services of the Roman Catholic Church, sung in Latin by unaccompanied voices, and consisting of single-line melody. Gregorian chant has existed since the Middle Ages. Gregory I, Pope from 590 to 604 AD, was believed to have organized the chants for use in the various services of the Church.

II. The CHURCH MODES. Gregorian chant is based on the *church modes*: a medieval system of eight scales which are different from the major and minor scales in current use. A chant encompasses the same approximate range as its related church mode.

| F = Final   D = Dominant |

1. Dorian (authentic)

(F)   (D)

2. Hypodorian (plagal)

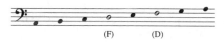

(F)   (D)

3. Phrygian (authentic)

(F)   (D)

4. Hypophrygian (plagal)

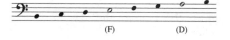

(F)   (D)

5. Lydian (authentic)

(F)   (D)   Continued

6. Hypolydian (plagal)

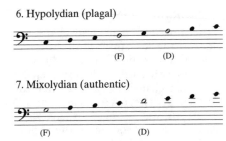

(F)   (D)

7. Mixolydian (authentic)

(F)   (D)

8. Hypomixolydian (plagal)

(F)   (D)

The *authentic* modes (1, 3, 5, and 7) are built up from, and usually end on, the *final* note (F). The *dominant* (D) or reciting tone, acts somewhat as a secondary tonal center and is used for reciting psalms. Melodic formulas based around reciting tones are called *psalm tones*.

III. See the modern system of modes at right: These modes occur in jazz, ethnic, and contemporary music.

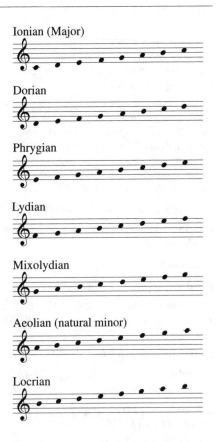

Ionian (Major)

Dorian

Phrygian

Lydian

Mixolydian

Aeolian (natural minor)

Locrian

---

gross [G., grohs], **grosso** [It., GROHS-soh] Large, great.

grosse caisse [F., grohs kehs], **grosse Trommel** [G., GROH-seh TROH-mel] Bass drum.

ground bass An unchanging, repeated bass pattern of four to eight measures, over which varying music is heard.

G-schlüssel [G., GEH-shlu(e)-sel] Treble (G) clef.

guaracha [Sp., gwah-RAH-cha] Cuban folk song.

guerriero [It., gwehr-ree-AY-roh] Martial, warlike.

güiro [GWEE-roh] Latin-American percussion instrument: a notched gourd which is scraped with a stick.

guitar There are two basic types of guitars – acoustic and electric. The acoustic guitar has a flat body with a long fretted neck. There are (usually) six strings which vibrate over a circular sound hole. The electric guitar may have a body similar in appearance to the acoustic guitar, or it may be carved from a single block of wood or other material; in either case, it is amplified (and often distorted) electronically. The guitar sounds one octave lower than written.

gusto, con [It., kohn GOOS-toh] Literally, "with taste." With style, zest.

H

H. 1. B natural (G.). (See *pitch names*.) 2. Abbr. for horn, hand.

habanera [Sp., ah-bah-NAY-rah] Cuban dance in moderate 2/4 meter. Its most common rhythm is: ♩♪♪ ♪♪♪

halb [G., hahlp] Half. *halbe Note* – half note; *halbe Pause* – half rest. See *notes*.

half-cadence A cadence which occurs at the end of the first half of a musical phrase, usually ending on the dominant; e.g. I-V, ii$_6$-V.

half-diminished seventh chord See *seventh chord (3)*.

half note, half rest See *notes*.

half step, half tone The smallest interval in Western music. On the keyboard, a half step is the closest key to the right or left of a given key.

half step   half step

hallelujah [Hebrew, hah-lay-LOO-yah] "Praise (ye) the Lord."

Hammerklavier [G., HAH-mehr-klah-veer] 19th-century name for the piano, used by Beethoven in his sonatas op. 101 and 106. (Op. 106 is nicknamed the "Hammerklavier Sonata.")

Handtrommel [G., HAHNT-troh-mel] Tambourine.

Harfe [G., HAHR-feh] See *harp*.

HARMONIC(S)

1. **Acoustics:** Musical instruments produce composite tones; that is, a number of pure tones sounding at the same time. Pure tones are called *harmonics*. The lowest harmonic is called the *fundamental*, or first harmonic. The frequencies of the other, higher harmonics are exact multiples of the fundamental frequency.

Harmonics above the fundamental are called *overtones*. The first overtone, therefore, is the second harmonic, and so on. The overtones produced above a fundamental are known as an *overtone series*. On the next page is an (incomplete) overtone series based on a fundamental C:

The relative strength of various harmonics in a tone is of critical importance in determining its *timbre* (sound "color").

2. **String playing:** When a string is touched at a *node* (exact fractional point), a higher flute-like tone, or harmonic, is produced. For instance, touching a string exactly in the center produces a tone an octave higher. Harmonics produced by lightly touching an open string are called *natural harmonics* and are indicated by a small circle:

Harmonics

1st overtone
(2nd harmonic)

fundamental
(1st harmonic)

A stopped string can also be touched lightly to produce a harmonic; such a tone is called an *artificial harmonic* and is notated as follows:

(♭●) - sounding pitch

← touched
← stopped

harmonica Mouth organ. It is a small, rectangular 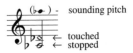 box with a row of openings on the side. Each opening is connected to a pair of reeds; one reed sounds when air is exhaled, the other when air is inhaled.

harmonic analysis The study of chords and harmonies in a composition, esp. as they relate to its structure.

harmonic interval See *interval*.

harmonic inversion See *inversion*.

harmonic minor scale See *minor scales*.

harmonic rhythm Rhythmic patterns which result from harmonic changes.

harmonium A small reed organ.

harmony 1. In a general sense, musical tones sounded simultaneously. Harmony can be thought of as the "vertical" element of a musical texture. (Also see *melody*.) 2. The combination of simultaneous notes in a chord. 3. The chordal structure of a musical composition.

harp; harpa [It., AHR-pah]; **harpe** [F., arp]; **Harfe** [G., HAHR-feh] A large stringed instrument with a vertical frame. The modern harp contains seven strings to the octave - C D E F G A B. Each string group (C's, D's, etc.) can be raised or lowered a half step by its corresponding pedal  (C pedal, D pedal, etc.). The harp has a 6 1/2 octave range; it is played by plucking the strings.

harpsichord A keyboard instrument in wide use before the piano. The action of the harpsichord causes strings to be plucked, rather than struck by hammers as with the piano.

hastig [G., HAHS-tikh] With haste, hurrying.

haupt- [G., haupt] Chief, principal. *Hauptstimme* - principal part; *Hauptwerk* - great organ.

haut(e) [F., oh, oht] High.

hautbois [F., oh-BWAH], **hautboy** [Eng., OH-boy] Oboe.

H dur [G., hah duhr] The key of B major.

head See *drum*.

head voice Higher register of a voice.

heftig [G., HEF-tikh] Violent, fierce.

heiter [G., HEI-ter] Cheerful, calm.

helicon A portable tuba used in marching bands.

hemidemisemiquaver (Brit.) 64th note. See *notes*.

hemiola 1. The ratio of 3:2. 2. In 6/4 meter, three half notes instead of two dotted half notes:

In 3/4 meter, this rhythm would be written:

hertz a unit of frequency equal to one cycle per second Abbr. Hz.
Also see *frequency*.

hervortretend [G., hehr-FOHR-treh-tant] Prominently, distinctly.

herzlich [G., HEHRTS-likh] Tenderly, heartfelt.

heterophony A type of polyphony where independent variations of the same melody are performed by two or more voices.

high pass filter See *electronic music*.

hi-hat See *drum set*.

His [G., hiss] B sharp. See *pitch names*.

HISTORY OF WESTERN MUSIC
At the bottom of this page is a table of musical periods, their approximate dates, and a few representative composers.

H moll [G., hah mohl] The key of B minor.

hocket A medieval contrapuntal device whereby the individual notes of a melody alternate between two voices, producing a "hiccuping" effect.

Hohlflöte [G., HOHL-flo(e)-teh] An organ flute stop with a powerful, "hollow" tone.

hold *Fermata*. ⌒

Holz [G., hohlts] Wood. *Holzblasinstrumente* - woodwinds; *Holzflöte* - "wood flute" - an organ stop; *Holzschlegel* - (wooden) drumstick.

homophony Music in which a melodic voice is supported by other voices in the same rhythm as the melody. See *polyphony*.

horn; Horn [G., hohrn] See *Brass Instruments (1)*.

huit [F., weet] Eight.

huitième de soupir [F., wee-tyehm deh soo-PEER] Thirty-second rest. See *notes*.

Humoreske [G., hoo-moh-RES-keh], humoresque [F., u(e)-moh-REHSK] A 19th-century instrumental composition, generally good-natured, often humorous.

PERIOD	TIME SPAN	REPRESENTATIVE COMPOSERS
medieval	850 - 1430	Machaut, Landini, de Vitry
renaissance	1430 - 1650	Dufay, des Prez, Palestrina, W. Byrd
baroque	1600 - 1750	J.S. Bach, Handel, Vivaldi, D. Scarlatti
classical	1750 - 1820	Mozart, Haydn, Beethoven
romantic	1820 - 1910	Schubert, Schumann, Chopin, Liszt, Wagner
impressionist	1890 - 1920+	Debussy, Ravel
20th century	1910 -	Schoenberg, Webern, Bartok, Stravinsky, Cage, Stockhausen

hurdy-gurdy A medieval instrument, mechanical in nature, whose strings are vibrated by means of a wheel turned by a hand crank.

hurtig [G., HOOR-tikh] Quick, nimble.

hyper- [Gr.] Higher (above, beyond).

hypo- [Gr.] Lower (below, beneath).

hypo-modes See *Gregorian chant*.

hymn A religious song of praise.

I

i [It., ee] The.

idillio See *idyll*.

idiomatic Appropriate for the technical and expressive resources of an instrument.

idiophones See *instruments*.

idyll; idylle [F., ee-DEEL]; **idillio** [It., ee-DEEL-yoh] A short, pastoral composition.

il [It., eel] The. *il più* – the most.

im [G., im] In the.

imitation In contrapuntal writing, the immediate restatement of a theme or a motif, in a different voice. *Canonic imitation* is the restatement of an entire voice part (see *canon*); *fugal imitation* is the restatement of a fugal subject.

immer [G., IM-mehr] Always, constantly.

impetuoso [It., im-pet-oo-OH-soh] Impetuous, hasty.

impressionism, impressionist period A style of music (and painting) which was in evidence in the late 1800's and early 1900's, especially in France. Claude Debussy (1862-1918) and Maurice Ravel (1875-1937) were its chief proponents. Impressionism has a vague, extremely subtle character, avoiding the tonal vocabulary of the romantic period which preceded it. Also see *History of Western Music*.

impromptu [F., eh(n)-PROH(N)P-tu(e) A 19th-century character piece in a somewhat casual style.

improvisation The creation of music as it is being performed. The ability to improvise is essential to popular idioms such as jazz and blues.

incidental music Music used to create atmosphere in a play or film, i.e., background music.

innig [G., IN-nikh] Intimate, heartfelt.

inno [It., IN-noh] Hymn.

input A signal fed into a circuit or device.

inquieto [It., in-kwee-EH-toh] Restless, uneasy.

instantemente [It., in-stahn-teh-MEN-tay] Insistently.

instrumentation 1. Orchestration. 2. The instruments used in a particular ensemble.

instruments Mechanisms for producing musical sounds, other than the human voice. Instruments may be grouped into five main categories:

  I. *Aerophones.* Wind instruments (woodwinds, brass).

  II. *Chordophones.* Stringed instruments (zither, dulcimer, harpsichord, clavichord, lute, koto, guitar, violin family, lyre, harp, piano).

  III. *Idiophones.* Percussion instruments (excluding drums) which are struck, shaken, plucked, or rubbed.

  IV. *Membranophones.* Drums.

  V. *Electrophones.* Sound source is generated electronically (electronic organ, synthesizer).

The pipe organ stands in a special category, but is closest to the aerophone family. Also see *brass instruments, percussion instruments, violin family, woodwind instruments*.

interlude 1. Music played between the acts of a play or between verses of a hymn or psalm. 2. Generic title for a short instrumental composition.

intermezzo [It., in-tehr-METS-tsoh] 1. Interlude. 2. Title for a 19th-century character piece, esp. by Schumann, Brahms.

INTERVAL

The distance in pitch between two tones, named according to the number of diatonic steps it includes:

An interval consisting of two *consecutive* tones is called a *melodic* interval:

An interval consisting of two *simultaneous* tones is called a *harmonic interval*:

UNISON (prime)	SECOND	THIRD	FOURTH	FIFTH	SIXTH	SEVENTH	OCTAVE (eighth)
It. prima	seconda	terza	quarta	quinta	sesta	settima	ottava
G. Prime	Sekunde	Terz	Quarte	Quinte	Sexte	Septime	Oktave
F. unisson	seconde	tierce	quarte	quinte	sixte	septième	octave

Intervals are identified not only by their number, but also by their quality – *perfect, major, minor, diminished, augmented*. The following table lists intervals according to quality, as well as the number of half steps that they contain.

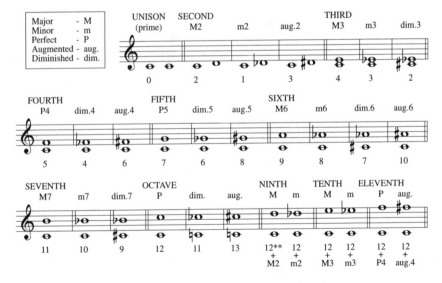

* intervals larger than an octave.

** 12 = octave

intimo [It., IN-tee-moh] Intimate. See *innig*.

intonation (It.) 1.The accurate production of pitch. 2. Playing in tune within an ensemble.

intrada [It., in-TRAH-dah] A festive or martial opening piece in a homophonic style.

intrepido [It., in-TREH-pee-doh] Intrepid, bold.

introduction A phrase or section preceding a composition.

Introit 1.The initial chant of the Mass, part of the Proper. See *Mass*. 2. A piece of music performed at the beginning of a church service.

invention A short piece in a freely contrapuntal style. J. S. Bach wrote a number of two and three-part inventions.

INVERSION

A change of position with respect to the notes of an interval or chord.

1. **Harmonic inversion.** Octave displacement of a note in an interval or chord. For example, the interval of a perfect fifth becomes a perfect fourth; a minor third becomes a major sixth, etc.

When a chord is "in first inversion," the third of the chord is the lowest note; when a chord is in second inversion, the fifth is the lowest note. Below is a root position triad and its possible inversions. (The arrows show the octave displacement.)

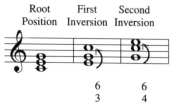

Root Position	First Inversion	Second Inversion
	6 3	6 4

Also see *seventh chord (1)*.

2. **Melodic inversion.** Changing each ascending interval into a corresponding descending interval, and vice versa, producing a "mirroring" effect.

Tonal inversion uses the degrees of the scale in the key in order to preserve the tonality:

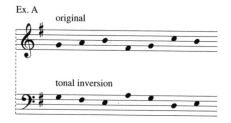

Ex. A — original — tonal inversion

Strict (real) inversion is an exact melodic inversion according to semitonal distance. In Ex. B below, the notes of Ex. A are given in strict inversion:

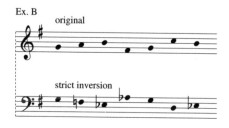

Ex. B — original — strict inversion

inverted canon Canon by means of *melodic inversion* (see *inversion*) or by retrograde motion.

inverted fugue Counterfugue. After the subject is stated initially, it enters in contrary motion (inversion) in the subsequent voice(s).

inverted mordent See *mordent*.

invertible counterpoint A passage of counterpoint in which the voices are exchanged, usually at the octave.

Applied to two voices, this technique is called *double* counterpoint; to three voices, *triple* counterpoint; to four voices, *quadruple* counterpoint.

Ionian mode See *Gregorian chant.*

irato [It., ee-RAH-toh] From "ira" (wrath). Angrily, passionately.

ironico [It., ee-ROH-nee-koh] Ironic.

istesso [It., ees-TEHS-soh] The same.

Italian sixth chord See *sixth chords.*

ite, missa est [L., EE-tay MEE-sah est] The final words of the Mass: "Go, it is the dismissal." See *Mass.*

J

Jagd [G., yahkt] Hunt. *Jagdborn* - hunting horn.

jam Jazz term for improvising.

jazz A style of 20th-century popular music originating in the United States. Jazz has always been a melting pot of various popular idioms. Early jazz was influenced by the blues and ragtime. (See *blues*; *ragtime*.) Jazz uses syncopated rhythms, as well as long-short patterns of eighths known as "swing":

$$ \text{♫} = \text{ca. } \overset{\lceil 3 \rceil}{\text{♩♪}} $$

A traditional jazz performance often starts with a melody played rather straightforwardly, followed by improvisations based on the same melody. In ensemble jazz, each cycle of the melody may involve a different soloist.

jeté (F.) See *bowing (6)*.

jeu [F., zheuh] 1. "Play, game." 2. Organ stop; *jeu de fonds* - foundation stop; *jeu à bouche* - flue stop; *jeu d'anche* - reed stop.

jeu de timbres [F., zheuh deuh TEH(N)BR] Glockenspiel.

jig See *gigue*.

jodel [G.] See *yodel*.

jota [Sp., HOH-tah] Spanish dance in fast triple meter.

Jubel [G., YOO-bel] Rejoicing, jubilation.

just intonation A system of tuning in which all intervals are derived from the pure perfect fifth and the pure major third. By "pure" we mean the interval ratios 3/2 for the perfect fifth and 5/4 for the major third.

This system is not in use today since modulation is impossible in just tuning. Also see *Pythagorean scale, equal temperament*.

K

K. See *Köchel*.

Kadenz [G., kah-DENTS] Cadence; cadenza.

Kammer [G., KAH-mehr] Chamber.

Kanon [G., KAH-non] Canon.

Kantate [G., kahn-TAH-teh] Cantata.

Kanzone [G., kahn-TSOH-neh] Canzona.

Kapelle [G., kah-PEL-leh] 1. Chapel. 2. Band, orchestra, church choir.

Kapodaster [G., kah-poh-DAHS-ter] *Capotasto*.

kazoo A small toy instrument played by humming.

Kesselpauke, Kesseltrommel [G., KEH-sel-pau-keh, KEH-sel-troh-mel] Kettledrum (timpano).

kettledrums Timpani.

key 1. The main note, or tonal center, of a composition. 2. Keyboard instruments: One of the levers which are depressed by the fingers to produce a tone. 3. Woodwind instruments: One of the levers used to open and close the holes of the instrument.

keyboard A bank of keys on pianos, harpsichords, organs, etc.

keynote Tonic.

KEY SIGNATURE

The sharps or flats at the beginning of each staff which indicate the key of a piece. A key signature may indicate either a major or a minor key, according to the following table:

Kind [G., kint] Child. *Kinderstück* - a piece for children.

Kirche [G., KEER-kheh] Church.

kithara [Gr., KITH-ah-rah] A stringed instrument of ancient Greece. Also see *lyre*.

klagend [G., KLAH-gent] Plaintive.

Klang [G., klahng] Sound, sonority. *Klangfarbe* - timbre.

Klangfarbenmelodie [G., KLAHNG-fahr-ben-meh-loh-dee] "Tone-color-melody." A term used by 20th-century composers of serial music to describe the practice of treating timbre as a structural element to be controlled. Also see *serial music*.

Klappe [G., KLAH-peh] One of the keys of a wind instrument.

klar [G., klahr] Clear, distinct.

Klarinette [G., klah-ree-NET-teh] Clarinet.

Klaviatur [G., klah-vee-ah-TOOR] Keyboard.

Klavier [G., klah-VEER] Piano (literally, "keyboard"). *Klavierstück* - piano piece.

klein [G., klein] Small. Of intervals: minor.

kleine Flöte [G., KLEI-neh FLO(E)-teh] Piccolo.

kleine Trommel [G., KLEI-neh TROH-mel] Snare drum.

klingend [G., KLING-ent] Sonorous, resonant.

Knabenchor [G., KNAH-ben-kohr] Boy's choir.

Knabenstimme [G., KNAH-ben-shtim-meh] A boy's voice.

Knarre [G., KNAHR-reh] Rattle.

Köchel [KO(E)-khel]Ludwig von Köchel compiled the catalogue listing of Mozart's works, abbr. K. (or K.V.). For example, K.545 designates the well-known "easy" piano sonata in C Major.

Kontrabass [G., KON-trah-bahs] Double bass.

Kontrafagott [G., KON-trah-fah-GOT] Contrabassoon.

Kontrapunkt [G., KON-trah-poonkt] Counterpoint.

Konzert [G., kon-TSEHRT] Concert; concerto.

Koppel [G., KOH-pehl] Coupler.

Kornett [G., kohr-NET] Cornet.

koto [KOH-toh] A Japanese stringed instrument (zither), with 13 strings, plucked with the fingers.

kräftig [G., KRA(E)F-tikh] Strong, vigorous.

Kreuz [G., kroyts] Sharp sign ♯.

Krummhorn [G., KROOM-hohrn] An instrument of the oboe family, with a capped reed mouthpiece, in use during the medieval and renaissance periods.

kurz [G., koorts] Short.

Kyrie [L./Gr., KEE-ree-ay] See *Mass*.

L

la See *pitch names*; *solmization*.

labial pipes Flue pipes.

Lage [G., LAH-geh] 1. Position; e.g., *erste Lage* – first position in string playing. 2. Chord position (open, close). 3. Vocal register.

lagnoso, lagrimoso, lamentoso [It., lahn-YOH-soh, lah-gree-MOH-soh, lah-men-TOH-soh} Mournful, lamenting.

lai See *lay*.

lancio, con [It., kohn LAHN-chee-oh] With vigor.

Ländler [G., LA(E)ND-lehr] A slow Austrian dance in 3/4 meter.

langsam [G., LAHNK-sahm] Slow.

languido [It., LAHN-gwee-doh] Languishing.

largamente [It., lahr-gah-MEN-tay] Broadly.

largando [It., lahr-GAHN-doh] Same as *allargando*.

larghetto [It., lahr-GET-toh] A little faster than *largo*.

largo [It., LAHR-goh] "Broad, wide." 1. Slow, dignified. 2. (cap.) A slow, dignified composition.

lauda [It., LAU-dah] Italian hymns of praise and devotion.

Laute [G., LAU-teh] Lute.

lay, lai A medieval song or ballad.

le [F., leuh] The.

leading tone, leading note The seventh degree of the scale, which "leads" (resolves) to the tonic. Also see *scale degrees*.

lebendig, lebhaft [G., lay-BEN-dikh, LEHP-haft] Lively.

leçon [F., leuh-SOH(N)] Lesson, exercise.

ledger lines Same as *leger lines*.

leere Saite [G., LEH-reh ZEI-teh] Open string.

legatissimo [It., lay-gah-TEES-see-moh] Very smooth and connected.

legato [It., lay-GAH-toh] Smooth, connected, with no interruption between notes.

Also see *bowing (1)*, *slur*.

Legende [G., leh-GEN-deh], **légende** [F., lay-ZHAH(N)D] A piece written in a romantic, narrative style.

léger [F., lay-ZHAY] Light, fast, buoyant.

leger lines Short lines drawn for notes too high or low to be placed on the staff.

leggero [It., layd-JAY-roh] Light, nimble, *léger*. Sometimes spelled as *leggiero*. Abbr. *legg.*

legni [It., LAY-nyee] Woodwind instruments.

legno [It., LAY-nyoh] Wood. *col legno* – see *bowing (special effects)*.

leicht [G., leikht] Light, easy.

leidenschaftlich [G., LEI-den-shahft-likh] Passionate.

leise [G., LEI-zeh] Soft.

leitmotif, Leitmotiv [G., LEIT-moh-teef] The technique used by Wagner and later operatic composers of representing characters, as well as recurring situations and ideas, by musical motifs.

Leiter [G., LEI-ter] 1. Scale. 2. Orchestra leader.

lent [F., lah(n)] Slow. *lentement* – slowly.

lentando [It., len-TAHN-doh] With increased slowness.

lento [It., LEN-toh] Slow.

lestezza [It., lehs-TET-TSAH] Agility, quickness.

lesto [It., LES-toh] Lively, nimbly.

libretto The text of an opera, oratorio, etc.

licenza [It., lee-CHEN-tsah] Freedom, license.

lieblich [G., LEEB-likh] Lovely, charming. *Liebeslied(er)* – love song(s).

Lied [G., leed(t)] A German song, esp. an art song, pl. *Lieder*.

lieto [It., lee-EH-toh] Joyful.

lieve [It., lee-EH-vay] Light, easy.

ligatures 1. Notational signs in use from the 13th- to the 16th-century. They are square symbols, combined to represent two or more notes. 2. The metal clamp used to fasten a reed to the mouthpiece of a woodwind instrument.

linke Hand [G., LEEN-keh hahnt] Left hand.

liscio [It., LEE-shoh] Smooth, even.

l'istesso tempo [It., lees-TES-soh TEM-poh] Maintain the same tempo; e.g., a change from 6/8 to 2/4 meter where the beat remains constant (♩. = ♩).

litany In the Roman Catholic Church, supplications which are sung responsively.

liturgy The rites and services of the Christian church, especially the Roman Catholic Church.

livre [F., leevr] Book.

livret [F., lee-VREH] Libretto.

liuto [It., lee-OOH-toh] Lute.

loco [It., LOH-koh] "Place." Return to the normal octave (after an 8va).

Locrian mode See *Gregorian chant III*.

lontano [It., lohn-TAH-noh] Distant, from afar.

lourd [F., loor] Heavy.

loure [F., loor] 1. Bagpipe (16th-17th c.) 2. 17th and 18th-century dance in slow to moderate 6/4 meter, with dotted rhythms – an optional movement of the suite. (See *suite*.) An example of a *loure* is found in Bach's French Suite No. 5.

louré (F.) See *bowing (7)*.

low pass filter See *electronic music*.

Luftpause [G., LOOFT-pau-zeh] Breathing rest.

lugubre [It., loo-GOO-bray] [F., lu(e)-GU(E)BR] Lugubrious, sad.

lullaby A cradle song, soft and gentle.

lunga [It., LOON-gah] 1. Long, sustained. 2. Long pause.

lusingando [It., loo-zeen-GAHN-doh] Caressing.

lustig [G., LOOS-tikh] Merry, cheerful.

lute A plucked stringed instrument of ancient origin, similar to a guitar, but with a body shaped like a halved pear.

lute harpsichord; Lautenwerk [G., LAU-ten-vehrk] A harpsichord with gut strings instead of metal ones. (Gut strings produce a softer tone.)

luttuoso [It., loot-too-OH-soh] Mournful.

Lydian mode See *Gregorian chant III.*

lyra 1. A stringed instrument of ancient Greece, a type of primitive harp, but played with a plectrum. (See *lyre.*) 2. Hurdy-gurdy. 3. Military glockenspiel.

lyre 1. Generic name for stringed instruments consisting of two arms connected at the upper end by a crossbar: *kithara, lyra,* crwth, kinnor. 2. A device for holding music while marching.

lyric opera See *opera.*

M

ma [It., mah] But. *ma non troppo* – but not too much.

madrigal A type of unaccompanied Italian vocal music of the 14th- and 16th-centuries. The madrigal in its final stage of development (i.e., by Monteverdi and Gesualdo) is polyphonic, imitative, elaborate, and often coloristic and dramatic.

maestoso [It., mah-es-TOH-soh] Majestic.

maestro [It., mah-EHS-troh] "Master." A title of respect for an eminent conductor, teacher, or composer.

maggiore [It., mah-JOH-ray] Major key.

Magnificat The canticle of the Virgin Mary.

main [F., meh(n)] Hand. *main droite* (m.d.) – right hand; *main gauche* (m.g.) – left hand. *à quatre mains* – for four hands.

majeur [F., ma-zheur] Major.

major With respect to intervals: greater, or larger. (See *intervals*.)

major key A key based on a major scale.

major scale A major scale – which is the principal scale of Western music – is a scale constructed according to the following pattern of whole steps (1) and half steps (1/2):

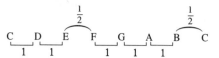

major triad A three-note chord comprised of a major third and a perfect fifth above the root. See *triad*.

malagueña [Sp., mah-lah-GAY-nyah] Popular song of Malaga, similar to a *fandango*.

malincónico [It., mah-leen-KOH-nee-koh] Melancholy.

manche [F., mah(n)sh]; **manico** [It., MAH-nee-koh] The neck of a violin or guitar. See *neck*.

mandolin A type of lute used chiefly in Italy. It has four (sometimes five) double *courses* (pairs) of steel strings. Mandolin playing is characterized by a rapid tremolo produced by a pick.

manica [It., MAH-nee-kah] Shift of position in violin playing.

maniera [It., mah-nee-AY-rah]; **manière** [F., ma-NYEHR] Manner, style.

Männerchor [G., MA(E)N-nehr-kohr] Men's chorus.

mano [It., MAH-noh] Hand. *mano destra* – right hand; *mano sinistra* – left hand.

manual One of the keyboards of an organ or harpsichord.

maracas [mah-RAH-kahs] A pair of shakers, usually made from gourds filled with seeds. Various types of maracas are common to Latin American and Caribbean music.

marcato [It., mahr-KAH-toh] Marked, stressed.

march; marche [F., marsh] Music which could be used for marching. Marches have a strong, simple rhythm and regular phrases. John Philip Sousa (1854-1932) is the best-known composer of marches for band.

marcia [It., MAHR-chee-ah] March. *alla marcia* - in the style of a march.

mariachi [Sp., mah-ree-AH-chee] 1. A type of Mexican street band, consisting chiefly of guitars. 2. A single member of a mariachi band.

marimba See *percussion instruments (4)*.

markiert [G., mahr-KEERT], **marqué** [F., mar-KAY] Strongly marked, accented.

Marsch [G., mahrsh] March.

martelé [F., mar-teuh-LAY], **martellato** [It., mahr-tel-LAH-toh] 1. See *bowing (3)*. 2. "Hammered" - forced, detached.

marziale [It., mahr-tsee-AH-lay] In the style of a march.

mask, masque A musical drama of the 16th and 17th centuries combining music, dance, and acting.

MASS

messa [It., MEH-sah]; **Messe** [F., mehs] [G., MEH-seh];

Missa [L., MEE-sah]

The service of the Roman Catholic Church which celebrates the Eucharist (Communion rite). The variable sections of the High Mass are called the Proper; the invariable sections, the Ordinary.

Below are the sung portions of the Mass, in the order of their performance:

Proper	Ordinary
Introit	
	Kyrie (Lord have mercy)
	Gloria [in excelsis Deo]
	(Glory to God in the highest)
Gradual	
Alleluia	
	Credo (I believe)
Offertory	
	Sanctus (Holy)
	Agnus Dei (Lamb of God)
Communion	
	Ite, missa est
	(Go, it is the dismissal)

As a musical composition, the Mass is a setting of the Ordinary: usually Kyrie, Gloria, Credo, Sanctus, Agnus Dei. These sections may be subdivided in larger works.

Some prominent examples of the Mass are: Giovanni Palestrina - Missa Papae Marcelli (Pope Marcellus Mass), 16th-c.; J. S. Bach - Mass in B Minor, 18th-c.; Ludwig van Beethoven - Missa Solemnis, 19th-c.

mässig [G., MA(E)S-sikh] Moderate.

mazurka [mah-ZER-kah] A Polish folk dance in triple meter. In serious music, the mazurka is best represented by Chopin.

measures Groups of beats, separated by bars. (See *bar*.)

mediant See *scale degrees*.

medieval period See *History of Western Music*.

medley A composition made up of a series of tunes.

mehr [G., mehr] More.

Meistersinger [G., MEIS-ter-zeen-ger] Member(s) of one of the German musical guilds of the 15th- and 16th-centuries, which continued the tradition of the *minnesingers*.

melisma Vocal passage sung on one syllable. "Melismatic" (several notes to a syllable) is the opposite of *syllabic* (one note to a syllable).

Gregorian chants are often characterized as melismatic or syllabic.

mellophone An E♭ instrument, similar to the French horn, used in marching bands.

melodia [It., may-loh-DEE-ah] Melody.

melodica A small wind instrument with a keyboard.

melodic interval See *interval*.

melodic inversion See *inversion*.

melodic minor scale See *minor scales*.

mélodie [F., may-loh-DEE] The French form of the German *Lied*.

melodrama Drama where spoken text is accompanied by background music.

melody A succession of musical tones, and therefore, the "horizontal" element of music, as opposed to *harmony* (simultaneous tones, or "verticality").

In order for a melody to have meaning, its tones must have rhythmic value. For this reason, it is impossible to separate melody and rhythm in real music.

melos [Gr., MAY-lohs] Song.

membranophones See *instruments*.

même [F., mehm] Same.

meno [It., MAY-noh] Less. *meno mosso* – less motion, less quickly.

Mensur [G., mehn-ZOOR] 1. *Scaling*. 2. Duration of a note.

mensural notation Notational system in use from 1250-1600. The system used single notes and *ligatures*.

mente, alla [It., AHL-lah MEN-tay] Improvised.

menuet [F., meuh-nu(e)-EH, **Menuett** [G., meh-noo-EHT] See *minuet*.

messa (It.), **Messe** (F.,G.) See *Mass*.

mesto [It., MES-toh] Sad, mournful(ly).

mesure [F., meuh-ZU(E)R] Measure, meter.

METER

A regular pattern of beats, which comprise measures. Meter is indicated by *time signatures* (e.g., 2/4, 4/4).

Simple Meters

Duple meter
Two beats per measure
(2/2 [¢], 2/4, 2/8)

Triple meter
Three beats per measure
(3/2, 3/4, 3/8)

Quadruple meter
Four beats per measure
(4/2, 4/4 [c], 4/8)

Compound Meters

Compound duple
(6/2, 6/4, 6/8)

Compound triple
(9/4, 9/8)

Compound quadruple
(12/4, 12/8, 12/16)

Quintuple, septuple meter

5/4, 5/8; 7/4, 7/8

metronome, metronome indications A device which clicks regular beats. The mechanical (non-electric) metronome consists of an inverted pendulum to which a sliding weight is attached. The position of the weight determines the number of oscillations per minute.

Metronome indications: M.M. stands for Maelzel's Metronome; therefore, the indication M.M.60 indicates that the tempo is 60 beats per minute. A more contemporary practice is to show tempo by a type of equation, e.g., ♩ = 60.

This indicates that the quarter note is the unit of beat and that there are 60 beats per minute.

mezza, mezzo [It., MET-tsah, MET-tsoh] Half, medium.

mezzo forte [It., MET-tsoh FOHR-tay] Medium loud.

mezzo piano [It., MET-tsoh pee-AH-noh] Medium soft.

mezzo-soprano See *voices, range of.*

mezza voce [It., MET-tsah VOH-chay] "Half voice." A lesser volume.

mi See *pitch names; solmization.*

microtone An interval smaller than a half step.

middle C The C nearest the middle of the piano keyboard.

MIDI Acronym for Musical Instrument Digital Interface, a type of digital code which allows synthesizers and computers to communicate with each other. For a complete discussion of MIDI and its related terms, see *electronic music.*

MIDI interface See *electronic music (simple sequencer setup).*

mineur [F., mee-NEUHR] Minor.

minim (Brit.) Half note. (See *notes.*)

minnesinger(s); Minnesänger [G., MIN-neh-zin-ger, MIN-neh-za(e)n-ger] German aristocratic poet-musicians, who were very important during the 12th- to the 14th-centuries. The minnesingers were influenced by the French *troubadours.*

minor With respect to intervals: lesser, or smaller. See *intervals.*

minore [It., mee-NOH-ray] Minor.

minor key A key based on a minor scale.

MINOR SCALES

There are three basic forms of minor scales.

I. **Natural minor.** The natural minor scale is built by spelling the major scale, beginning with the 6th degree:

C Major: C D E F G **A B** C

A Natural Minor: **A B** C D E F G

The scale is called "natural" because no accidentals (sharps, flats, or naturals) are needed to construct the scale.

The pattern for the natural minor scale is as follows:

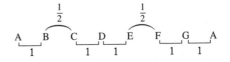

II. **Harmonic minor.** The harmonic minor scale is built by raising the 7th degree of the natural minor scale:

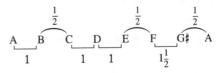

III. Melodic minor. The melodic minor scale is built by raising both the 6th and 7th degrees of the natural minor scale:

Note: The descending form of the melodic minor scale is the same as the natural minor scale.

Relative minor, relative major. Minor scales share the same key signature as their related major scales. For instance, A Minor is the *relative minor* of C Major; conversely, C Major is the *relative major* of A Minor. For a listing of major keys and their related minor keys, see *key signature.*

minor seventh chord See *seventh chord (2).*

minor triad A three-note chord comprised of a minor third and a perfect fifth above the root. See *triad.*

minstrel 1. A medieval musician, esp. one who sang or recited poetry while accompanying himself with a stringed instrument. 2. Vaudeville performer.

minuet; minuetto [It., men-oo-EHT-toh]; **menuet** [F., meuh-nu(e)-EH]; **Menuett** [G., meh-noo-EHT] 1. A French country dance, first introduced at the court of Louis XIV in 1650, in moderate 3/4 meter. 2. A movement of the baroque suite. (See *suite*.) 3. During the classical period, the third movement of most symphonies. Such a movement contains a *trio*. (See *trio – 3.*) Also see *symphony.*

Missa (L.) See *Mass.*

misterioso [It., mees-teh-ree-OH-soh] Mysteriously.

misura [It., mee-ZOO-rah] Measure, beat. *alla misura* – in strict time; *senza misura* – without strict time.

mit [G., mit] With.

mixer A device for combining several input signals. Mixers allow the control of each input volume, as well as the combined input volume.

Mixolydian mode See *Gregorian chant III.*

modal Of or relating to modes, or to harmonies based on modes.

modality The use of modal melodies or harmonies in a composition.

mode In a broad sense, the term means: Any pattern of notes arranged in a scale. For a listing of modes, see *Gregorian chant.*

moderato [It., moh-deh-RAH-toh], **modéré** [F., moh-day-RAY] A moderate tempo, between andante and allegro.

modifier A synthesizer function which alters signals produced by a controller or control voltage source.

modulation 1. Change of key within a composition. 2. Acoustics: The process in which a waveform is periodically varied. See *amplitude modulation*; *frequency modulation.*

modulation wheel See *electronic music.*

module See *electronic music; sound module.*

moins [F., mweh(n)] Less.

moll [G., mohl] Minor.

molto [It., MOHL-toh] Much, very.

monitor A device for checking audio signals, esp. during recording.

monody An unaccompanied solo song.

monophony Music consisting of pure melody, without any accompaniment. Also see *polyphony.*

monotone Singing on an unchanging pitch.

morceau [F., muhr-SOH] Composition, piece.

mordant Variant spelling of *mordent*.

mordent A musical ornament, consisting of the written note and the note a diatonic step below; it is begun on the beat.

With the *inverted mordent*, the added note is a diatonic step *above* the written note:

morendo [It., moh-REN-doh] Fading away.

mosso [It., MOH-soh] Moved, agitated; movement, motion. *meno mosso* – less movement; *più mosso* – more movement.

motet 1. An unaccompanied choral work written for the Roman Catholic Church, based on a sacred Latin text. Various forms of the motet were composed from the 13th-18th-centuries. 2. Modern usage: Unaccompanied choral work based on a sacred text.

motif, motive A short, recognizable figure that recurs throughout a passage or piece. The motif is a unifying element within a work.

MOTION

I. The patterns of pitch in a melody, i.e., ascending or descending.

II. The melodic relationship of two or more voice parts:

Parallel motion.
    Movement in the same direction, where the interval between the two voices remains the same (Ex. 1).

Similar motion.
    Movement in the same direction, where the interval between the two voices changes (Ex. 2).

Contrary motion.
    Movement in opposite directions (Ex. 3).

Oblique motion.
    One part stays on the same pitch (Ex. 4).

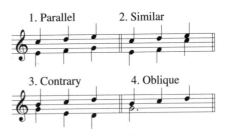

moto [It., MOH-toh] Motion. *andante con moto* – a little faster than *andante*.

mouth organ *Harmonica*.

mouthpiece The part of a wind instrument which comes into contact with the player's mouth. There are four basic types:

1) Cupped   (brass instruments)
2) Single-reed (clarinets, saxophones)
3) Double-reed (oboes)
4) Fipple   (recorders)

mouvement [F., moov-MAH(N)]; **movimento** [It., moh-vee-MEN-toh] Movement; tempo.

movable do See *solmization.*

movement Main section of a larger work such as a sonata, symphony, or suite. Several movements comprise a complete work.

multi-timbral module See *sound module; electronic music.*

multi-track See *track.*

munter [G., MOON-ter] Lively, cheerful.

musette; musetta [It., moo-ZET-tah} 1. French bagpipe. 2. Dance piece with a drone accompaniment. For an example of a musette, see Bach's English Suite No. 3, the gavotte.

music; musica [L., MOO-zee-kah] The organization of sound for aesthetic or expressive purposes.

music box A machine with a turning metal cylinder studded with pins. Tones are produced when the pins come into contact with a row of metal teeth. Today inexpensive "music boxes" produce a sound characteristic of a traditional music box by means of a small computer chip programmed to play a single tune.

music-drama See *opera.*

musicology The scholarly study of music; musical scholarship.

music therapy Use of music in the treatment of physical, emotional, and/or psychological problems.

musique concrète [F., mu(e)-ZEEK koh(n)-KREHT] In electronic music, music which is made by altering and/or combining recorded sounds, as opposed to electronic music, which is produced by purely electronic means. As a compositional technique, it refers mainly to splicing pieces of magnetic tape together to create unusual effects.

muta [It., MOO-tah] An indication to change the tuning, e.g., of timpani.

mutation pipes See *foot.*

mute A device for muffling the sound of an instrument. 1. Violins: A clamp attached to the bridge. The mute is called for by the phrase *con sordini.* 2. Brass: Mutes come in a variety of sizes and shapes – they are inserted into the bell of the instrument. 3. Timpani: Timpani are muted with a cloth.

mutig [G., MOO-tikh] Courageous, spirited.

N

nach [G., nahkh] After.

Nachahmung [G., NAHKH-ah-moong] Imitation.

nachdrücklich [G., NAHKH-dru(e)k-likh] Emphatic, energetic, vigorous.

nachlassend [G., NAHKH-lahs-sent] Relaxing, slackening.

Nachschlag [G., NAHKH-shlahg] The two notes that usually follow the end of a trill.

notated:

played:

Nachspiel [G., NAHKH-shpeel] Postlude.

Nachtmusik [G., NAHKHT-moo-zeek] "Night-music"; serenade.

Nachtstück [G., NAHKHT-shtu(e)k] "Night-piece"; nocturne.

natural 1. The sign ♮, which cancels a preceding sharp or flat. 2. A note not affected by an accidental.

natural harmonic See *harmonic (2)*.

natural horn A horn which has no keys or valves, capable of producing only natural tones. (See *natural tones*.)

natural minor scale See *minor scales*.

natural tones In wind instruments, harmonics produced by overblowing (proper control of breath and lips). For example, a pipe with a fundamental of C can produce harmonic tones such as C C G C E G B♭ C D E without the use of valves. (See *harmonics*.)

Neapolitan sixth chord See *sixth chord*.

neben [G., NAY-ben] Next to; secondary.

neck That part of a violin, guitar, etc. which is held by the player and to which the fingerboard is attached.

negligente [It., nay-glee-JEN-tay] "Negligent"; unconstrained.

neighboring tone, neighbor tone See *nonharmonic tones I (2)*.

neoclassicism A style of 20th-century music which incorporates baroque and classical forms and techniques into contemporary idioms.

nera [It., NEH-rah] Quarter note. (See *notes*.)

neu [G., noy] New.

neuf [F., neuf] Nine.

neun [G., noyn] Nine.

neume(s) Medieval notational sign(s) used to notate plainsong, such as Gregorian chant.

nicht [G., nikht] Not.

ninth See *interval*.

ninth chord A chord which contains the interval of a 9th above the root; e.g., C-E-G-B-D.

nobile [It., NOH-bee-lay] Noble, dignified.

nocturne "Night piece." Typically, a romantic work for the piano with a lyrical melody over a broken-chord accompaniment. Chopin wrote a large number of nocturnes for the piano; Debussy wrote an orchestral work in three movements entitled *Nocturnes*. The title is still in use today.

node See *harmonic (2)*.

noel, noël [F., nuh-EHL] A Christmas carol, hymn.

Noël [F., nuh-EHL] Christmas.

noire [F., nwahr] Quarter note. (See *notes*.)

noise Undesired sound.

noise generator A synthesizer device which produces unpitched sound (noise).

non [It., nohn] Not, no.

nonet Chamber piece for nine instruments.

NONHARMONIC TONES

A general term for ornamental tones which are not part of the harmony at the moment when they occur. There are two main categories, *rhythmically weak* and *rhythmically strong*:

I. Rhythmically weak nonharmonic tones. Occur *between* two harmonic tones.

1. **Passing tones.** Fill in a melodic skip (Ex. 1).

2. **Auxiliary tone** (neighboring tone). Ornaments a stationary tone. An *upper auxiliary* goes upward by a half or whole step and then returns (Ex. 2A); a *lower auxiliary* goes downward and then returns (Ex. 2B).

3. **Anticipation.** Anticipates the note of resolution; i.e., the note of resolution is the same as the nonharmonic tone (Ex. 3).

4. Both the **échappée** [ay-sha-PAY] (escape tone) and the **cambiata** ornament a melodic second. With the *échappée*, the motion of the ornamenting tone is *contrary* to that of the melodic second. The échappée is preceded by a step and resolves by a skip (usually a 3rd) (Ex. 4A).

With the *cambiata*, the motion of the ornamenting tone is *similar* to that of the melodic second. It is preceded by a skip and resolves by a step (Ex. 4B).

II. Rhythmically strong nonharmonic tones. The general term for this category is **appoggiatura**. An appoggiatura occurs on the beat, and it is a half step or a whole step above or below the tone of resolution (Ex.'s 5A & 5B).

A **suspension** is an appoggiatura prepared by a tie (Ex. 6).

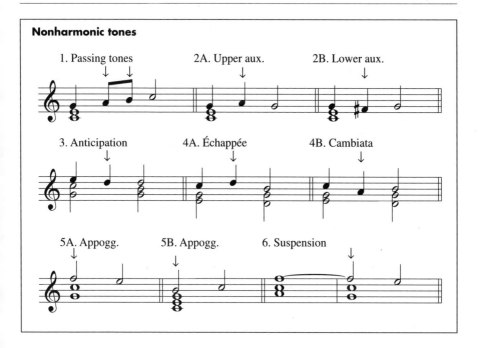

Nonharmonic tones

1. Passing tones 2A. Upper aux. 2B. Lower aux.

3. Anticipation 4A. Échappée 4B. Cambiata

5A. Appogg. 5B. Appogg. 6. Suspension

non troppo [It., nohn TROHP-poh] Not too much.

notation Method(s) used for writing down music.

NOTES The signs with which music is written on a staff. See table on the next page.

notturno [It., noht-TOOR-noh] 1. Nocturne. 2. Type of 18th-century *serenade*.

nove [It., NOH-vay] Nine.

nuance Subtle difference(s) in articulation, phrasing, etc.

nut See *frog*.

Table of Note and Rest Values

WHOLE NOTE O	**WHOLE REST** ▬
semibreve (Brit.)	
semibreve (It.)	pausa di semibreve (It.)
ronde (F.)	pause (F.)
ganze Note (G.)	ganze Pause (G.)
HALF NOTE	**HALF REST** ▬
minim (Brit.)	
bianca (It.)	pausa di bianca (It.)
blanche (F.)	demi-pause (F.)
halbe Note (G.)	halbe Pause (G.)
QUARTER NOTE	**QUARTER REST**
crotchet (Brit.)	
nera (It.)	pausa di nera (It.)
noire (F.)	soupir (F.)
Viertel (G.)	viertel Pause (G.)
EIGHTH NOTE	**EIGHTH REST**
quaver (Brit.)	
croma (It.)	pausa di croma (It.)
croche (F.)	demi-soupir (F.)
Achtel (G.)	achtel Pause (G.)
SIXTEENTH NOTE	**SIXTEENTH REST**
semiquaver (Brit.)	
semicroma (It.)	pausa di semicroma (It.)
double-croche (F.)	quart de soupir (F.)
Sechzehntel (G.)	sechzehntel Pause (G.)
THIRTY-SECOND NOTE	**THIRTY-SECOND REST**
demisemiquaver (Brit.)	
biscroma (It.)	pausa di biscroma (It.)
triple-croche (F.)	huitième de soupir (F.)
Zweiunddreissigstel (G.)	zweiunddreissigstel Pause (G.)
SIXTY-FOURTH NOTE	**SIXTY-FOURTH REST**
hemidemisemiquaver (Brit.)	
semibiscroma (It.)	pausa di semibiscroma (It.)
quadruple-croche (F.)	seizième de soupir (F.)
Vierundsechzigstel (G.)	vierundsechzigstel Pause (G.)

O

o As a symbol, a circle has several meanings: 1. Above a note, a *harmonic*. 2. Beside a note, an open string (guitar). 3. After a chord symbol or interval, *diminished*.

obbligato [It., ohb-blee-GAH-toh] 1. Obligatory, not to be omitted, as opposed to *ad libitum* (omissible). 2. A melodic part subordinate to the solo in a composition.

ober [G., OH-ber] Over, above.

Oberton [G., OH-behr-tohn] Overtone. See *harmonic*.

Oberwerk [G., Oh-behr-vehrk] Swell organ.

Obligat [G., oh-blee-GAHT] Obbligato.

obligato Incorrect spelling of *obbligato*.

obligé [F., oh-blee-ZHAY] Obbligato.

oblique motion See *motion*.

oboe [E., It., G.], **oboi** [It. pl., oh-BOH-ee] See *woodwind instruments (3)*.

ocarina An egg-shaped instrument, with a mouth-hole and finger holes.

octave See *interval*.

octave signs When the octave signs *8va——* or *8——* appear above notes, play them an octave higher than written; when they appear below notes, play an octave lower. For two octaves, the number *15* (not 16) is used.

octet 1. A musical composition for eight instruments. 2. A group of eight musicians.

Odhecaton [od-HEK-ah-ton] The earliest printed publication of polyphonic music, published by Petrucci in 1501.

œuvre [F., euvr] Opus.

Offertory 1. See *Mass*. 2. Music which accompanies the offering in a religious service.

Office, Divine In the Roman Catholic liturgy, the service of the canonical or daily hours, celebrated eight times a day:

1) Matins	– after midnight
2) Lauds	– at sunrise
3) Prime	– 6 a.m.
4) Terce	– 9 a.m.
5) Sext	– noon
6) None	– 3 p.m.
7) Vespers	– sunset
8) Compline	– before retiring

ohne [G., OH-neh] Without.

Oktave [G., ohk-TAH-veh] Octave. *Oktavflöte* – piccolo; *Octavfagott* – contrabassoon.

ondeggiando [It., ohn-day-JAHN-doh], **ondulé** [F., oh(n)-du(e)-LAY] For violins, etc., a special type of *tremolo*, created by an undulating movement of the bow. Indicated by

Ondes Martenot An early electronic instrument (ca.1928) capable of producing single tones and glissandi. It has been used by 20th-century composers such as Varèse and Messiaen, and by film composers, esp. in science-fiction and horror movies.

onze [F., oh(n)z] Eleven.

op. Abbr. for *opus*.

open diapason An organ stop of the principal family.

open fifth A triad without the third (C-G).

open notes, open tones 1. See *natural tones*. 2. Tones produced on *open strings*.

open position See *close position*.

open strings On stringed instruments, strings which are not stopped by the finger. Indicated by a small circle placed above (or below) the note.

OPERA

Oper [G., OH-per]

A large-scale dramatic work for voices, performed on a stage with scenery and costumes, with orchestral accompaniment. An opera usually consists of *recitatives*, *arias*, and *choruses*.

On the next page is a table outlining some general styles of opera, and some representative composers. (Styles which are not by definition comic or serious are placed between the two categories.)

Some general observations can be drawn from the table:

For much of its development, opera may be classified into two main categories: *comic opera* and serious opera *(opera seria)*. Comic opera is a general term for comic or light opera which usually has a happy ending and often contains spoken dialogue. Serious opera, on the other hand, deals with heroic or tragic situations; it is usually sung throughout, consisting of recitative and aria.

The Italian style of comic opera is *opera buffa*. (The French *opéra bouffe* was a light, popular style of comic opera.) In France, the term *opéra comique* was used to describe an opera which contained spoken dialogue, regardless of whether it was comic or tragic.

The 19th-century saw the development of *grand opera*, which was a predominantly Italian movement (Rossini, Bellini, Verdi). *Lyric opera* (Gounod) contained elements of both grand opera and opéra comique. In Germany, Wagner created a new style of *music-drama*, where instead of distinct arias, there is a continuous musical unfolding. Wagner used the *leitmotiv* technique to unify the dramatic and musical elements of his operas.

In the late 19th-century, a style of opera appeared which is sometimes known as *verismo* ("verity"), in which ordinary people are depicted in familiar situations. The musical language of *verismo* is that of the late 19th-century – large ensembles, dramatic expression, and dissonant or exotic colors.

The *expressionist* (early 20th-century), atonal style of Alban Berg has found few imitators. The majority of modern operatic composers prefer to work in a neo-classic or "neo-romantic" style.

Since the 1980's the composers Philip Glass and John Adams have achieved considerable success with their "minimalist" operas; in a different vein, John Corigliano's *Ghosts of Versailles* with its eclectic contemporary style has also met with critical acclaim.

COMIC	SERIOUS	COMPOSER	TYPICAL WORK
	18TH CENTURY		
opera buffa		Mozart	...Figaro (1786)
	opera seria	Handel	Rodelinda (1725)
ballad opera (Eng.)		John Gay	The Beggar's Opera (1728)
	19th CENTURY		
	grand opera	Rossini	Guillaume Tell (1829)
		Meyerbeer	Les Huguenots (1836)
opera buffa (It.)		Rossini	The Barber of Seville (1816)
	Italian	Bellini	Norma (1831)
	(continuation	Verdi	Otello (1887)
	of grand opera)		
	opéra comique (F.)	Bizet	Carmen (1875)
		Massenet	Manon (1884)
opéra bouffe		Offenbach	Orpheus (1875)
		J. Strauss	Die Fledermaus (1874)
	lyric opera	Gounod	Faust (1859)
	romantic (G.)	Weber	Die Freischütz (1821)
	music-drama (G.)	Wagner	Tristan und Isolde(1859)
	verismo	Leoncavallo	Pagliacci (1892)
	late romantic	Puccini	La Bohème (1896)
	20th CENTURY		
atonal (expressionism)		Berg	Wozzeck (1925)
"traditional"		Britten	Peter Grimes (1945)
minimalist		Glass	Einstein on the Beach (1976)

opéra bouffe See *opera.*

opera buffa See *opera.*

opera seria See *opera.*

operetta [It., oh-peh-RET-tah] A short, light opera.

opus (L.) Work. With a number, used to indicate the order, often chronological, of a composer's works.

oratorio A composition based on a long, narrative, religious text. There are vocal solos, ensembles, and choruses, with instrumental accompaniment. Often a narrator is used.

Orchester [G., ohr-KEHS-ter] Orchestra.

ORCHESTRA

The symphony orchestra consists of four basic groups of instruments: winds, brass, percussion, and strings. In addition to these groups, special instruments such as organ, piano, or mandolin are added occasionally.

The following table shows the approximate numerical strength of the classical orchestra of Mozart and Haydn, versus the modern orchestra. Note that this table also shows the typical arrangement, from top to bottom, of the instruments in an orchestral score:

	CLASSICAL ORCHESTRA	MODERN ORCHESTRA
Woodwinds		
Piccolo	-	1
Flute	2	2 or 3
Oboe	2	2 or 3
English Horn	-	1
Clarinet	2	2 or 3
Bass Clarinet	-	1
Bassoon	2	2 or 3
Contrabassoon	-	1
Brass		
Horn	2	4-6
Trumpet	2	3 or 4
Trombone	-	3 or 4
Tuba	-	1
Percussion		
Percussion	2 (timp.)	4 or more
Harp	-	1 or 2
	(approximate)	
Strings		
1st Violins	8-10	12-18
2nd Violins	6-8	10-16
Violas	4-6	8-12
Cellos	3-6	6-10
Double Basses	2-4	6-8

Names of Orchestral Instruments

English	Italian	French	German
WOODWINDS	**LEGNI**	**BOIS**	**HOLZBLAS-INSTRUMENTE**
piccolo (Picc.)	flauto piccolo (ottavino)	petite flûte	kleine Flöte
flute (Fl.)	flauto	flûte	Flöte
oboe (Ob.)	oboe	hautbois	Oboe (Hoboe)
English horn (E.H.)	corno inglese	cor anglais	englisches Horn
clarinet (Cl.)	clarinetto	clarinette	Klarinette
bass clarinet (B.Cl.)	clarinetto basso	clarinette basse	Bassklarinette
bassoon (Bsn.)	fagotto	basson	Fagott
contrabassoon (C. Bsn.)	contrafagotto	contrebasson	Kontrafagott
BRASS	**OTTONI**	**CUIVRES**	**BLECH-INSTRUMENTE**
horn (Hrn., Hn.)	corno	cor	Horn
trumpet (Tpt.)	tromba	trompette	Trompete
trombone (Tbn.)	trombone	trombone	Posaune
tuba (Tuba)	tuba	tuba	Tuba (Basstuba)
PERCUSSION	**PERCUSSIONE** (Batteria)	**BATTERIE**	**SCHLAGZEUG**
timpani (Timp.) (kettledrums)	timpani	timbales	Pauken
snare drum (S.D.)	tamburo	tambour (militaire) (caisse claire)	kleine Trommel
bass drum (B.D.)	(gran) cassa	grosse caisse	grosse Trommel
cymbals (Cym.)	piatti	cymbales	Becken
triangle (Tri.)	triangolo	triangle	Triangel
tambourine (Tamb.)	tamburino (tamburo basco)	tambour de basque	Schellentrommel (Tamburin)
gong (tam-tam)	tam-tam	tam-tam	Tam-tam
harp	arpa	harpe	Harfe
STRINGS	**ARCHI**	**CORDES**	**STREICH-INSTRUMENTE**
violin (Vl., Vln.)	violino	violon	Violine, Geige
viola (Vla.)	viola	alto	Bratsche
(violon) cello (Vc.)	violoncello	violoncelle	Violoncell
double bass (D.B., C.B.)	contrabasso	contrebasse	Kontrabass

orchestra bells Glockenspiel. See *Percussion Instruments - 2.*

orchestration The art of writing music for performance by an orchestra, with regard to its technical, musical, and sonorous capabilities.

ordinario [It., ohr-dee-NAH-ree-oh] Ordinary, normal.

Ordinary See *Mass.*

organ chorale A polyphonic composition for organ based on a chorale melody.

organ, pipe An instrument with one or more keyboards, as well as pedals for producing bass tones. Sound is produced by the vibration of air in pipes of various sizes. Also see *organ pipes.*

In the electronic organ, sound is produced by means of *oscillators* or digital sampling (see *sampler*) rather than pipes.

ORGAN PIPES

There are two classes of organ pipes: *flue* and *reed.*

I. Flue pipes. Air passes through a narrow slit or "flue."

  1. *Principal.* Produces a "full organ" sound.

  2. *Flute.* The fundamental and odd harmonics are emphasized.

  3. *String.* Viola, cello, salicional, gamba.

II. Reed pipes. Air sets a metal reed or tongue into vibration then passes through a resonator.

  1. *Chorus.* Trumpet family

  2. *Orchestral; solo.* Wind family (bassoon, clarinet, etc.)

Also see *stopped pipes; foot.*

organ point Pedal point.

organum The earliest type of polyphonic music, from the 9th- through the 12th-centuries, consisting of a *plainsong* tenor to which contrapuntal parts are added.

Orgel [G., OHR-gel], **orgue** [F., uhrg] Organ.

ornaments Notes used to embellish a melody. See *acciaccatura, appoggiatura, Bebung, grace note, mordent, nonharmonic tones, trill, turn.*

oscillation See *vibration.*

oscillator In electronic music, the basic sound-producing device, which produces simple waveforms. See *electronic music.*

ossia [It., ohs-SEE-ah] Indication for an alternate way of playing a passage.

ostinato [It., ohs-tee-NAH-toh] A recognizable pattern that is continuously repeated. Also see *ground bass.*

ôtez, ôter [F., oh-TAY] Take off, e.g., a stop or mute.

ottava [It., oht-TAH-vah] Octave. Abbr. *8va* or *8. All' ottava, ottava alta, ottava sopra, 8va* or *8* (above notes): play one octave higher than written. *Ottava bassa (8vb), ottava sotto, 8va* or *8* (below notes): play one octave lower than written.

ottavino [It., oht-tah-VEE-noh] Piccolo.

otto [It., OHT-toh] Eight.

ottoni [It., oht-TOH-nee] Brass (instruments).

output A signal that comes out of a circuit or device.

overblowing See *natural tones.*

overtone, overtone series See *harmonic.*

overture An instrumental composition written to introduce an opera, oratorio, etc.

P

pacato [It., pah-KAH-toh] Calm.

pandiatonicism The use of the diatonic scale in 20th-century music, but without its traditional implications (for example, functional harmony).

pan pipes, panpipes, pandean pipes, Pan's pipes A wind instrument of ancient origin, made of pipes  of graded sizes fastened together, stopped at the bottom and blown into at the top.

pan-pot A device which is capable of moving a sound within a stereo field, e.g., from left to right.

pantomime The art of expressing dramatic action silently, by means of body movement and facial expression.

pantonality Term used to describe late 19th-c.–20th-c. music which shifts among key centers without actually becoming atonal.

parallel fifths, octaves In part writing, the duplication of a melodic interval at the fifth or octave, which is to be avoided in strict counterpoint.

parallel intervals A succession of like intervals.

parallel keys (parallel major, parallel minor) A major and a minor key with the same tonic, e.g., C Major and C Minor.

parallel motion See *motion*.

paraphrase 1. In early music, the free elaboration of a plainsong melody. 2. A transcription or arrangement, with variations.

parlando, parlante [It., pahr-LAHN-doh, pahr-LAHN-tay] "Speaking." 1. In singing, an indication to approximate speech. 2. In instrumental music, expressive, eloquent.

parlato [It., pahr-LAH-toh] "Spoken." In comic opera: spoken rather than sung.

parody Mass A type of 15th–16th-c. Mass which contains material borrowed from a chanson, madrigal, or motet.

part 1. The music for a single instrument or voice within a larger work, e.g., the clarinet *part*. 2. A single melodic line of a contrapuntal composition. 3. A section of a composition.

partial Harmonic.

partita [It., pahr-TEE-tah] 1. Variation. 2. Suite, e.g., the keyboard and violin "Partitas" by J. S. Bach.

partition [F., par-tee-SYOH(N), **Partitur** [G., pahr-tee-TOOR], **partitura** [It., pahr-tee-TOO-rah] A score, full score.

part song A choral piece with the melody in the top voice. It is homophonic, not polyphonic. Also see *glee*.

pas [F., pah] Dance; step.

passacaglia [It., pahs-sah-KAHL-yah] A type of *chaconne*: a variation form based on a continuous *ostinato*, usually in the bass.

passage A short section or phrase in a composition.

passacaille, passecaille [F., pa-sa-KAY, pa-seuh-KAY] Passacaglia.

passepied [F., pas-PYAY] An 18th-century French dance in lively 3/8 or 6/8 meter, and an optional movement of the suite. (See *suite*.)

passing tone See *nonharmonic tones I (1)*.

passionato; passione, con [It., pahs-syah-NAH-toh, kohn pahs-SYOH-nay] Passionately, fervently.

pasticcio [It., pah-STEE-choh], **pastiche** [F., pas-TEESH] A composition using work of more than one composer, e.g., an operatic medley.

pastorale A composition which suggests rural life, esp. the pipes of shepherds.

patch See *electronic music (sound module)*.

patetico [It., pah-TEH-tee-koh], **pathetisch** [G., pa-TEH-tish] With great emotion.

Pauken [G., PAU-ken] Timpani.

pausa [It., PAU-sah] Rest. See *notes*.

pause [F., poz] Whole rest. See *notes*.

pavane A slow, stately dance originating in the 16th century, usually in 4/4 or 4/2 meter.

peak The highest (or lowest) point of a sound wave.

PEDAL

I. A mechanism controlled by the feet, such as a piano or organ pedal. The modern grand piano has three pedals:

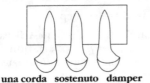

una corda   sostenuto   damper

The *damper pedal* lifts all of the dampers, allowing the strings to ring. This pedal allows the sound to continue, even when the fingers lift off the keys. The *una corda* ("one string") pedal – loosely called the "soft" pedal – shifts the keyboard action so that the hammers strike only two of the three unison strings in the treble range, and only one of the two unison strings in the tenor range. Thus the volume is reduced, and the timbre is changed as well. The *sostenuto pedal* will sustain only those tones which are sounded by the keys already being depressed. It is especially effective for pedal points.

II. The term "pedal" is a short term for *pedal point*.

---

pedal harp Another term for the modern harp.

pedal harpsichord A harpsichord equipped with a bass pedal-board similar to those of the organ.

pédalier [F., pay-da-LYAY] The pedal board of the organ.

pedal point A bass note which is sustained for a long time while harmonies change in the upper parts.

pedal tone A *fundamental* tone. (See *harmonic*.)

pentatonic scale A scale having five tones to the octave. The most common type can be built by omitting the 4th and 7th degrees of the major scale, e.g., C-D-E-G-A-C. Such a scale can begin on any of the five tones, e.g., E-G-A-C-D-E. The black keys of the piano can also be used to form pentatonic scales.

per [It., pehr] For, by, in, through.

percussion Instruments which are struck, shaken, or rubbed. See *instruments (III, IV)*; *percussion instruments*.

PERCUSSION INSTRUMENTS

The percussion instruments commonly found in the orchestra are listed below. Other instruments more rarely used are listed as separate headings in this dictionary.

INSTRUMENTS OF DEFINITE PITCH

1. **Timpani** (kettle-drums). Standard orchestral instrument consisting of a metallic basin with a calf-skin or plastic head stretched over it. The tension on the head is  controlled by a foot pedal, allowing for quick changes in pitch. Most orchestras have three or four timpani.

Range by size

sounds as notated

2. **Glockenspiel** (orchestra bells). An instrument consisting of steel bars attached to a frame and played with small mallets. It has a bright, ringing tone.

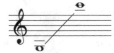

sounds 2 octaves higher

3. **Xylophone.** The wooden bars of the xylophone are arranged in a keyboard pattern. Vertical tubes are hung underneath the bars to increase their resonance. The tone is hard and piercing. Played with hard mallets.

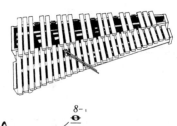

sounds 1 octave higher

4. **Marimba.** A larger form of the xylophone, with a warm, mellow tone. Played with mallets.

sounds as notated

5. **Vibraphone** (vibraharp). Instrument similar to the marimba, but with metal bars and electrically driven propellers under each bar. The speed of the propellers can be adjusted to create varying rates of vibrato.

The vibraphone is most often associated with "cool" jazz.

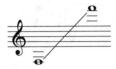

sounds as notated

6. Chimes (tubular bells, orchestral bells). A set of large metal tubes arranged in a keyboard pattern and vertically suspended in a frame. Struck with wooden hammers.

sounds as notated

7. Crotales (antique, or finger cymbals). Very small pairs of cymbals, tuned to a definite pitch. They produce a delicate bell tone.

sounds 2 octaves higher

INSTRUMENTS OF INDEFINITE PITCH

8. Snare drum (side drum). A small cylindrical metal drum with two heads. Snares (wire strings) are stretched across the bottom head, and they are responsible for its raspy sound. Played with sticks.

9. Tenor drum. Deeper and larger than the snare drum, and having no snares.

10. Bass drum. A two-headed drum of great size and power, played with a padded beater.

11. Tambourine. A small wooden hoop with a single head attached to it. "Jingles" (metal disks) are attached to openings cut in the hoop. The tambourine is either shaken or struck.

12. Triangle. A small steel bar bent into a triangular shape, struck with a small metal beater.

13. Cymbals. Large, circular, convex brass plates. *crash cymbals* – a pair of cymbals struck together; *suspended cymbal* – played with soft beaters for *rolls*, delicate tones, etc.

14. Gong (tam-tam). Large circular piece of metal, struck with a soft beater. It has great dynamic range and power, and a long resonating time.

Also see *drum set (kit)*. For listings of orchestral percussion instruments in Italian, French, and German, see *orchestra*.

perdendosi [It., pehr-DEN-doh-see] Dying away; gradually decreasing in tempo and volume.

perfect cadence See *cadence.*

perfect intervals Intervals of the fourth, fifth, and octave; so called because of the "perfection" of their tone. Also see *intervals.*

perfect pitch Also known as *absolute pitch.* The ability to recognize the actual pitch of any note heard, without any prior reference. Also see *relative pitch.*

period 1. A complete musical "sentence," usually consisting of an antecedent and a consequent phrase, and ending with a cadence. (See *antecedent and consequent.*) 2. An historical epoch in music, e.g., the romantic "period." Also see *History of Western Music.*

permutation See *serial music.*

pesante [It., peh-SAHN-tay] Heavy, ponderous.

petit [F., peuh-TEE] Little, small.

petite flûte [F., peuh-TEET flu(e)t] Piccolo.

peu [F., peuh] Little, not much. *un peu* – a little, somewhat; *peu à peu* – little by little.

pezzo [It., PET-tsoh] Piece, composition.

Pfeife [G., PFEI-feh] Fife; organ pipe.

phase distortion Changes in the harmonic structure of a sound wave.

phrase A logical division of a melody; a succession of tones which together comprise a musical idea. It may consist of only a few notes or continue for several measures. Also see *antecedent and consequent.*

Phrygian mode See *Gregorian chant III.*

piacere, a [It., ah pyah-CHAY-ray] See *a piacere.*

piacevole [It., pyah-CHAY-voh-lay] Pleasing, agreeable.

pianamente [It., pyah-nah-MEN-tay] Smoothly, softly.

pianissimo [It., pyah-NEES-see-moh] Abbr. *pp.* Very soft.

pianississimo [It., pyah-nees-SEES-see-moh] Abbr. *ppp.* Very, very soft.

piano [It., PYAH-noh] Abbr. *p* . Soft.

piano, pianoforte The original name for the piano was *pianoforte.* The term *piano-forte* ("soft-loud" in Italian) is a descriptive one, since the piano was the first stringed keyboard instrument capable of producing a wide dynamic range.

There are two types of modern pianos – *upright* and *grand.* With grand pianos, the strings are stretched above a horizontal soundboard. The largest size is full or *concert* grand (9 feet), ranging down to the baby grand (5 feet or less). With upright pianos, the strings and soundboard are vertical. The keyboard action is also considerably less complicated. There are several types of upright pianos: the studio upright (ca. 46" high), the console (ca. 40" high), and the spinet (ca. 36" high).

Also see *pedal.*

piano-forte Abbr. *pf.* A dynamic marking for *piano,* followed immediately by *forte.*

piano quartet An ensemble consisting of piano, violin, viola, and cello.

piano trio See *trio (3).*

piano quintet Chamber music group consisting of piano and string quartet.

piatti [It., PYAHT-tee] Cymbals.

Picardy third In a minor key: a major third used in the final chord – primarily a baroque practice.

piccolo See *woodwind instruments (1).*

pick A small flat object used to pluck the strings of a guitar, mandolin, etc. Also called *plectrum.*

pickup, pick-up One or more notes immediately before a bar, which begin a melodic phrase. Also called *anacrusis, upbeat.*

pieno [It., PYAY-noh] Full. *a voce piena* – with full voice.

pietà [It., pyay-TAH] Pity.

Pikkolo (flöte) [G., PEE-koh-loh (FLOE-teh)] Piccolo. The modern name is *kleine Flöte.*

pincé [F., peh(n)-SAY] "Pinched." 1. Plucked, pizzicato. 2. Mordent.

pipe 1. An early type of recorder. 2. See *organ pipes.*

pipe organ See *organ, pipe.*

pistons 1. Spring valves used on brass instruments. (See *valve.*) 2. Devices on organs for making quick stop changes.

pitch The "highness" or "lowness" of a tone, measured according to its frequency. (See *frequency.*) The modern standard of pitch is A = 440 (cycles/second), A being the A above middle C on the piano keyboard.

pitch bend wheel See *electronic music (keyboard controller).*

PITCH NAMES

The following table gives the names for the tones of an octave:

English

| C | D | E | F | G | A | B |

German

| C | D | E | F | G | A | H |

French

| ut | ré | mi | fa | sol | la | si |

Italian; Spanish

| do | re | mi | fa | sol | la | si |

Note that in German, "H" stands for B (H moll = B minor); whereas, "B" stands for B♭ (B moll = B♭ minor).

Pitches may be named flat or sharp according to the following table:

English	flat	sharp
	double-flat	double-sharp
German	- es	- is
	- eses	- isis
French	bémol	dièse
	double-bémol	double-dièse
Italian	bemolle	diesis
	doppio bemolle	doppio diesis

For example, *ut bémol* (F.) = C flat; *fa diesis* (It.) = F sharp.

German uses the suffix *- es* for flat and the suffix *-is* for sharp. Therefore, the German names of the altered pitches are:

C♭	C♯	D♭	D♯	E♭	E♯	F♭
Ces	Cis	Des	Dis	Es*	Eis	Fes

F♯	G♭	G♯	A♭	A♯	B♭	B♯
Fis	Ges	Gis	As*	Ais	B*	His

*irregular forms

For double-flats and double-sharps, use -*eses* for ♭♭ and -*isis* for ♯♯, after the letter name. For example, *Cisis* = C♭♭. The irregular forms are *Eses* (E♭♭) and *Ases* (A♭♭). And since "B" stands for B♭, *Bes* = B♭♭.

Naming pitches by octave

A standard for naming pitches by octave now exists as a result of computer music notation programs: C3 represents middle C on the piano keyboard, followed in ascending order by C4, C5, C6, and C7. C2 represents the octave below middle C, followed in descending order by C1 and C0. The (incomplete) octave below C0 is represented by -1. Therefore the lowest note on the standard-size piano is A-1.

Pitches falling between these octave names share similar numerical designations. For example, G2 is the G below middle C; A3 is the A above middle C, etc.

This method effectively replaces the older method of naming pitches by octave, shown below:

New method:
C-1 C0 C1 C2 C3 C4 C5 C6

Old method:
C" C' C c c' c" c''' c''''

pitch pipe A small device used mainly for giving the pitch for a choir.

più [It., pew] More. *più forte* – louder; *più mosso* – more movement (faster).

pivot chord A chord used for modulation – it is common to both the initial and the new key.

pizzicato [It., peet-tsee-KAH-toh] Abbr. *pizz.* For instruments of the violin family, an indication to pluck rather than bow the strings, Canceled by *arco* (bowed).

placido [It., PLAH-chee-doh] Calm, tranquil.

plagal cadence See *cadence.*

plagal mode See *Gregorian chant.*

plainchant See *plainsong.*

plainsong The monophonic and free melody (chants) of ancient liturgies, of which *Gregorian chant* is a principal type. Other types are Ambrosian, Gallican, and Mozarabic.

plaqué [F., pla-KAY] Struck at once (non-arpeggiated).

player piano A piano with a mechanism that allows the instrument to play itself. Originally, performances were encoded onto paper rolls which directed the mechanism; modern player pianos use tape cassettes or disks.

plectrum 1. See *pick.* 2. The part of the harpsichord action which plucks the string.

plein-jeu [F., pleh(n)-ZHEUH] Full organ.

plus [F., plu(e)s] More.

pochetto [It., poh-KET-toh] Very little.

poco [It., POH-koh] Little. *poco a poco* – little by little, gradually. *un poco* – a little.

poi [It., poy] Then, afterward.

point The upper end of the violin bow.

point d'orgue [F., pweh(n duhrg] 1. Fermata. 2. Pedal point. 3. Cadenza.

polka A lively Bohemian dance in duple meter.

polonaise 1. A stately, festive Polish dance in triple meter. Its characteristic rhythm is

Chopin wrote a number of polonaises.

2. A movement of a suite. (See *suite.*)

poly- Many, diverse.

polyphony Music which has several individual voice-parts; contrapuntal music. Polyphony contrasts with *monophony*, which is a single melody line, and *homophony*, where the voice-parts do not have individual rhythms – they provide harmonic support for the melody.

polyrhythm The use of "cross rhythms" – for example, three against two – or different meters simultaneously.

polytonality The simultaneous use of two or more chords or keys. See *bitonality.*

pomposo [It., pohm-POH-soh] Pompous, grand.

ponderoso [It., pohn-dehr-OH-soh] Ponderously, heavily.

ponticello [It., pohn-tee-CHEHL-loh] The bridge of stringed instruments. *sul ponticello* – see *bowing (special effects – 1).*

port MIDI connector. See *electronic music.*

portamento [It., pohr-tah-MEN-toh] In singing, gliding gradually from one tone to the next. The effect may also be called for on the violin or trombone.

portato [It., pohr-TAH-toh] Halfway between legato and staccato. Also see *bowing (7).*

Posaune [G., poh-ZAU-neh] Trombone.

positif [F., poh-zee-TEEF], **Positiv** [G., poh-zee-TEEF] Abbr. *pos.* 1. "Chair" organ; movable organ. 2. Organ manual that resembles a smaller organ.

position 1. See *close position.* 2. In violin playing, positions are places on the fingerboard where the hand shifts to play higher or lower tones, e.g., 1st, 2nd, 3rd positions. 3. The placement of the trombone slide. There are seven positions available.

possibile [It., pohs-SEE-bee-lay] Possible.

postlude Music played at the conclusion of a religious service.

potentiometer Abbr. *pot.* Technical term for the volume control on audio equipment.

potpourri [F., poh-poo-REE] Medley.

pour [F., poor] For.

poussé, poussez [F., poo-SAY] Upbow.

praeludium [L., pray-LOO-dee-oom] Prelude.

precipitando [It., pray-chee-pee-TAHN-doh] Rushing, impetuous.

preciso [It., pray-CHEE-zoh] Precise, exact.

prelude 1. An introductory section or movement. (In the keyboard music of J.S. Bach, the prelude is as important as the fugue which follows.) 2. A non-descriptive title used by Chopin and others for instrumental solo music, usu-

ally piano. 3. Music played at the beginning of a religious service.

premiere The first public performance of a composition.

prepared piano A piano whose sound is changed by inserting bolts, clips, strips of rubber, etc., between the strings. First used by the composer John Cage.

pressante [It., prehs-SAHN-tay], **presser** [F., preh-SAY] "Press." – urgent, hurrying.

prestissimo [It., preh-STEES-see-moh] As fast as possible.

presto [It., PREH-stoh] Very fast; faster than *allegro.*

prima [It., PREE-mah] 1. Unison. 2. First.

prima donna (It.) The singer of the principal female role of an opera. The term may also refer to a conceited or temperamental performer.

primary accent Downbeat.

prima volta, seconda volta [It., PREE-mah VOHL-tah, say-KOHN-dah VOHL-tah] The 1st and 2nd endings of a repeated section, abbr. as

1. and 2.

prime; Prime [G., PREE-meh] 1. Unison. (See *intervals.*) 2. First note of a scale.

primo [It., PREE-moh] Principal, first. In piano duets, the first or upper part is labeled *primo*; the second or lower part, *secondo.*

principal 1. The diapason family of a pipe organ. 2. The first chair in an instrumental section of an orchestra or band.

principale See *concerto grosso.*

program, program change See *sound module; electronic music.*

program music See *absolute music.*

progression A succession of intervals (melodic progression) or chords (harmonic progression).

pronunziato [It., proh-noon-tsee-AH-toh] Pronounced.

Proper See *Mass*.

proportional notation 1. Mensural notation. 2. Same as *spatial notation*.

proposta [It., proh-POHS-tah] The subject of a fugue.

prosa [L., PROH-zah], **prose** [F., prohz] Sequence.

psalm 1. A musical setting of a text from the Book of Psalms. 2. A sacred song or hymn.

psalm tone See *Gregorian chant II*.

Psalter The Book of Psalms, translated into the native language of a country, and used for congregational singing.

psaltery An ancient type of zither, played by plucking the strings.

pulse Beat.

punta, punto [It., POON-tah, POON-toh] Point. *a punto d'arco* – with the point of the bow.

Pythagorean scale A diatonic scale whose tones are all derived from the perfect fifth, according to the ratio 3/2. The scale is said to have been invented by Pythagoras (550 B.C.). It is of historical importance in the development of tuning systems. Also see *equal temperament; just intonation*.

Q

quadrille [F., ka-DREEY] A 19th-century French dance, in five sections, for four couples moving in a square.

quadruple counterpoint See *invertible counterpoint*.

quadruple-croche [F., kwah-DRU(E)PL-kruhsh] Sixty-fourth note. (See *notes*.)

quadruple meter See *meter*.

quadruplet A group of four notes, played in the time of three.

quality As applied to intervals, whether they are perfect, major, minor, diminished, or augmented. See *interval*.

quantization A process where rhythms are rounded off to a pre-designated rhythmic value. See *electronic music*.

quart de soupir [F., kart deh soo-PEER] Sixteenth rest. See *notes*.

quarta [It., KWAHR-tah], **quarte** [F., kart], **Quarte** [G., KVAHR-teh] Interval of a fourth.

quartal harmony Harmony based on the fourth rather than the usual system of thirds (tertian harmony). Typical chords based on fourths are: C-F-B♭, D-G-C. These harmonies can be heard in much of the music of Paul Hindemith (1895-1963), as well as in most jazz since bebop.

quarter note, quarter rest See *notes*.

quarter tone An interval equal to one-half semitone. There are 24 quarter tones to the octave. Quarter tones are important in some avant-garde music, and in non-Western music.

quartet, Quartett [G., kvahr-TET], **quartetto** [It., kwahr-TET-toh] 1. A musical composition for four instruments. 2. A group of four musicians. See *piano quartet; string quartet*.

quasi [It., KWAH-zee] In the manner or style of.

quatre [F., katr], **quattro** [It., KWAHT-troh] Four.

quatuor [F., kwah-tu(e)-UHR] Quartet.

quaver (Brit.) Eighth note. (See *notes*.)

quick-step Military term for a lively march.

quieto [It., kwee-EH-toh] Quiet, calm.

quindecima [It., kween-DAY-chee-mah], A fifteenth. Two octaves higher (or lower). Abbr. *15ma*.

quinta [It., KWEEN-tah], **quinte** [F., keh(n)t], **Quinte** [G., KVIN-teh] Interval of a fifth.

quintet; Quintett [G., kvin-TET]; **quintetto** [It., kwen-TET-toh] ; **quintette** [F., keh(n)-TEHT] 1. A musical composition for five instruments. 2. A group of five musicians. See *string quintet; piano quintet*.

quintina [It., kwen-TEE-nah] Quintuplet.

Quintole [G.] , **quintolet** [F., keh(n)-toh-LEH] Quintuplet.

quintuor [F., keh(n)-TOOR] Quintet.

quintuple meter See *meter*.

quintuplet A group of five equal notes played in the time of four.

R

rabab Arabic term for a bowed lute of ancient origin. There are several types in use in the Middle East and North Africa.

rāga [RAH-gah] The melodic formulas used in the classical music of India.

ragtime A style of early 20th-century popular piano music which flourished around 1915, and which experienced a revival in the 1970's. In ragtime, the right hand plays syncopated melodies, while the left hand accompanies in "stride" style (a low bass note followed by a chord).

ralentir [F., ra-lah(n)-TEER] To slow down.

rallentando [It., rahl-len-TAHN-doh] Abbr. *rall.* Same as *ritardando*.

range The span between the highest and lowest notes playable on an instrument or produced by a singer. For instrumental ranges, see *brass instruments; percussion instruments;* the *violin family; voices, range of;* and *woodwind instruments*.

rank A complete set of organ pipes of the same type, usually arranged in a row.

rap African-American popular music style in which lyrics are spoken instead of sung.

rapidamente [It., rah-pee-dah-MEN-tay] Rapidly.

rasch (G.) Swift, hasty, rash.

ratchet, Ratsche (G.) A percussion instrument made of a cogged wheel turned by a handle, against which rubs a mounted strip of wood or metal. Produces a loud rattling sound.

rattenuto [It., rah-ten-NOO-toh] Holding back.

rattle A gourd filled with pebbles or seeds; played by shaking.

re; ré (F.) See *pitch names; solmization*.

real answer See *fugue*.

rebec [REE-behk] Ancient bowed stringed instrument derived from the *rabab*. It is pear-shaped, usually with three strings.

recapitulation See *sonata form*.

recessional Music played or sung at the close of a religious service.

recht [G., rehkht] Right (as opposed to *left*).

récit [F., ray-SEE] Vocal solo piece (France, 17th-18th c.).

Récit [F., ray-SEE] Swell manual of a French organ.

recital A public performance by one or two performers.

recitative; recitativo [It., ray-chee-tah-TEE-voh] The speech-like singing of text in a rhythmically free manner, used in narrative sections of opera.

recorder A straight wooden flute with a whistle mouthpiece and usually eight finger holes. It has a round tone. There are four sizes of the modern recorder: soprano, alto, tenor, and bass.

redowa [RED-oh-wah]A waltz of Bohemian (Czech) origin, similar to the *mazurka*.

reduction 1. In French: arrangement. 2. A solo version, usually for piano, of an orchestral, choral, etc., composition. Often used for rehearsal purposes.

reed 1. In woodwind instruments: A thin strip of cane, being the part of the mouthpiece which vibrates. There are two types: *single* and *double*. On single reed instruments (clarinet, saxophone), the reed is attached to the mouthpiece by a clamp (ligature). On double reed instruments (oboe, bassoon), two reeds are joined together to form an oval opening. Also see *woodwind instruments*.

2. Metal reeds are used in the harmonica, harmonium, accordion, and in organ reed stops. These can produce only one pitch, determined by their length. Also see *organ pipes*.

reed organ A small organ whose sound is produced by the vibration of metal reeds (no pipes). The harmonium is a type of reed organ.

reed pipes See *organ pipes*.

reel A lively Scotch/Irish dance. In North America it is known as the "Virginia reel." See *strathspey*.

refrain The section of a song which is repeated after each verse. Also called *chorus*, esp. in popular and gospel music.

reggae Jamaican popular music style, influenced by American soul music. Bob Marley (1945-1981) and his group, the Wailers, is typical of the style.

register 1. Organ: A full set of pipes controlled by one stop. Harpsichord: A *choir* of strings controlled by one lever (or pedal). 2. A portion of the range of an instrument or voice, e.g., "head voice," "chest voice," etc.

registration Organ and harpsichord: The combination of stops and couplers used in the performance of a work. May be indicated, or left to the performer's discretion.

related keys Keys sharing the same key signature.

relative major, relative minor See *minor scales*.

relative pitch The ability to recognize (or sing) an interval after hearing a given pitch. See *perfect pitch*.

release In electronic music, the cessation of sound within an *envelope*. See *envelope; electronic music*.

religioso [It., ray-lee-JOH-soh] Religiously.

remettez [F., reuh-meh-TAY] Organ: Take off a stop.

renaissance period See *History of Western Music*.

renforcer [F., rah(n)-fuhr-SAY] "Reinforce" – get louder.

repeated measure The sign ⁄ is used to indicate one or more repeated measures.

repeated notes See *tremolo*.

repeat sign Music which is enclosed by the two signs is to be repeated.

replica [It., RAY-plee-kah] Repeat.

reprise [E.], [F., reuh-PREEZ]; **Reprise** [G., reh-PREE-zeh] 1. Repeat. 2. Refrain. 3. Recapitulation.

Requiem Mass A musical setting of the Mass for the Dead (Missa pro defunctis).

resin See *rosin*.

resolution The progression of a dissonant note or chord to a consonant one.

resonance The transmission of vibrations from a vibrating body (sound source) to another body (*resonator*). A resonator vibrates at the same frequency as the sound source affecting it, which is why this phenomenon is also called *sympathetic vibration.*

The effect of resonance is to reinforce or prolong a sound; in fact, the term *resonant* is used to convey a sense of richness or fullness. Also see *resonator* below.

resonator For a definition, see *resonance.* Resonators provide natural amplification. Some resonators of musical instruments are: 1) the belly of a guitar, violin; 2) the tubes beneath the bars of a xylophone. In organ pipes, that part of the pipe which amplifies the edge tone (flue pipe) or the metallic vibration (reed pipe) into a full-bodied organ sound.

response 1. A choral reply. 2. An "amen" sung by a choir.

rest Silence, pause. (See *notes.*)

ressortir [F., reuh-suhr-TEER] To emphasize.

restatement Recapitulation. See *sonata form.*

resultant tone Same as *combination tone.*

retardation A suspension which resolves upward.

retenu [F., reuh-teuh-NU(E)] Restrained, held back.

retrograde Backward motion of a melody, beginning with the last note and proceeding to the first note. Other terms for retrograde are *cancrizans, crab motion.* Retrograde is an important feature of twelve-tone music. See *serial music.*

retrograde inversion The combination of retrograde and inversion, achieved by playing a melody backward while simultaneously inverting it. See *serial music.*

reveille Military wake-up call, played on a bugle. From réveil [F.]: waking.

reverberation, reverb Repetitions or echoes of sound that are spaced so closely together that they cannot be distinguished individually. The longer the delay in repetition, the greater the feeling of depth or space.

rhapsody; rhapsodie [F., rap-soh-DEE]; **Rhapsodie** [G., rap-zoh-DEE] Composition in a free, romantic style.

rhumba Rumba.

rhythm Musical movement in time, especially in the sense of units or patterns which may be divided or grouped together.

rhythm and blues Also known as R & B. A term used by the recording industry to describe popular music originally oriented to the African-American audience.

ribs The sides of violins, etc.

ricercar(e) [It., ree-chehr-KAHR] Any of various instrumental forms, esp. of the 16th- or 17th-century, in an imitative style. The most important example of this form is the organ ricercar, which is characterized by the development of a single theme in an imitative style, and by passages in toccata style.

ricochet See *bowing (6).*

ridotto [It., ree-DOHT-toh] "Reduced," arranged.

riduzione [It., ree-doo-tsee-OH-nay] Arrangement.

rigaudon, rigadoon A 17th-century French dance, and an optional movement of the suite.

rigo [It., REE-goh] Staff.

rigore [It., ree-GOH-ray] "Rigor." Strict tempo.

rim The round metal edge of a drum. *rim shot* – a powerful percussive stroke on a snare drum. One stick is laid across the rim and/or is in contact with the head, while the other stick strikes the middle of the resting stick.

rinforzando [It., reen-fohr-TSAHN-doh] Abbr. *rinf.* "Reinforced." Accent on individual note(s) or chord(s).

ring modulation Two sound sources modulating each other, producing the sums and differences of the two while eliminating the originals. Ring-modulated sounds are "metallic" in quality. See *electronic music.*

ripienista [It., ree-pyeh-NEES-tah] An orchestral player.

ripieno, ripieni [It., ree-PYEH-noh, ree-PYEH-nee] "Full." The full (tutti) orchestra rather than the soloists (e.g., violino di ripieno). *senza ripieni* – the *concertino* only. See *concerto grosso.*

riposato [It., ree-poh-SAH-toh] Calm, reposed.

riprendere [It., ree-PREN-day-ray] Resume the original tempo.

ripresa [It., ree-PRAY-sah] 1. Repeat, repetition. 2. Recapitulation. Same as *reprise.*

risoluto [It., ree-soh-LOO-toh] Bold, resolute.

risposta [It., rees-POHS-tah] The answer of a fugue.

risvegliato [It., ree-zvayl-YAH-toh] Awakened, animated.

ritardando [It., ree-tahr-DAHN-doh] Abbr. *rit.* Becoming slower. Commonly known as "ritard."

ritenuto [It., ree-tay-NOO-toh] Slower, held back.

ritmo [It., REET-moh] Rhythm.

ritornello [It., ree-tohr-NEL-loh], **ritournelle** [F., ree-toor-NEHL] 1. In the 17th century, an instrumental conclusion

to an operatic song or aria. Occasionally it may precede the song (aria). 2. The tutti sections of a concerto grosso movement.

robusto [It., roh-BOOS-toh] Firm, bold.

rock American-European popular music which began in the 1960's as a development of rock 'n' roll. There are a number of different styles of rock: folk-rock, hard rock (now called heavy metal), alternative rock, etc.

rock 'n' roll American popular music style of the 1950's and early 1960's. Basic rock 'n' roll is sung in 4/4 and is accompanied by amplified or electric guitars (and sometimes piano or organ). Important contributors to rock 'n' roll are: Chuck Berry, Little Richard, Jerry Lee Lewis, and Elvis Presley.

rococo [roh-koh-KOH] An artistic movement of the 18th century characterized by ornate decoration, prettiness, and elegance. Its musical representatives include Couperin, Telemann, and D. Scarlatti.

Rohr [G., rohr] Reed. *Rohrblattinstrumente* – reed instruments; *Rohrflöte* – chimney flute (organ); *Rohrwerk* – reed stops (organ).

Röhrenglocken [G., RO(E)-ren-glok-en] Chimes. Literally, "pipe-bells."

roll A drum sound sustained by means of rapidly alternating strokes. In a "buzz" roll, each stroke consists of several bounces of the stick.

romance [F., ruh-MAH(N)S] 1. A short, lyrical song. 2. (G.) A lyrical, tender, instrumental composition.

romanticism, romantic See *History of Western Music.*

romanza [It., roh-MAHN-tsah], **Romanze** [G., roh-MAHN-tseh] Same as *romance.*

ronde [F., roh(n)d] Whole note. (See *notes*.)

rondeau [F., roh(n)-DOH] 1. An important song form of medieval and renaissance music (and poetry). It contains a partial refrain in the middle and a complete refrain at the end. 2. French term for a composition featuring the alternation of a main section with subordinate sections, like a *rondo*.

rondo A classical form used in sonatas, symphonies, and concertos. It consists of a recurring theme ("rondo") and several intermediate episodes, e.g., *A* B *A* C *A* B *A*.

root The fundamental note of a chord. Also see *triad*.

root position A chord in which the root is the lowest note. See *inversion*.

rosin, resin The substance applied to the hair of the violin bow to increase its friction (grip).

roulade [F., roo-LAHD] 1. Vocal melisma; florid melody. 2. Fast ornamental passing notes linking two main melody notes.

round A canon in which each voice sings the melody over and over, while the entrances are staggered. A well-known example of a round is "Row, Row, Row Your Boat."

row Tone row. See *serial music*.

rubato [It., roo-BAH-toh] Subtle variations in tempo for dramatic or expressive purposes.

ruhig [G., ROO-ikh] Quiet, calm.

Rührtrommel [G., RU(E)R-trom-mel] Tenor drum.

rumba [Sp., ROOM-bah] A highly syncopated Cuban dance, performed by instrumentalists and a singer.

run A rapid embellishing passage.

rustico [It., ROOS-tee-koh] Rural, pastoral.

sackbut The medieval trombone.

Saite [G., ZEI-teh] String. *Saiteninstrument* – stringed instrument.

salicional See *organ pipes*.

salmo [It., SAHL-moh] Psalm.

saltando, saltato [It., sahl-TAHN-doh, sahl-TAH-toh] Same as *sautillé*. See *bowing (4)*.

saltarello [It., sahl-tah-REL-loh] A lively Italian dance, in a skipping style.

samba A Brazilian folk dance in syncopated 2/4 meter.

sample and hold A synthesizer controller which produces quantized variations of a waveform.

sampler A MIDI device which can record a sound digitally. After a sound has been digitally recorded (sampled), it can be played on any key of a synthesizer or controller. Sampled sounds can also be stored as preset sounds in modules, enabling composers and performers to mimic the sounds of all available acoustic instruments. See *electronic music*.

Sanctus [L., SAHN(K)-toos] See *Mass*.

sanft [G., zahnft] Soft, gentle.

sans [F., sah(n)] Without.

sarabande A slow, dignified dance in 3/4 meter, and a standard movement in the baroque suite. (See *suite*.)

sarrusophone A brass instrument with a double reed; not in common use.

sassofone [It., sahs-soh-FOH-nay] Saxophone.

Satz [G., zahts] 1. A movement of a composition. 2. Style.

sautillé See *bowing (4)*.

sawtooth wave Waveform consisting of a fundamental and all harmonics, their intensity being inversely related to frequency $(1, 1/2, 1/3, 1/4$, etc.). See *electronic music*.

saxophone A single-reed wind instrument with a curved metal body and a conical bore. The four principal types have the same written range, but are pitched differently.

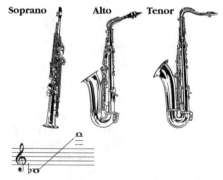

		sounds	
B♭	*Soprano*	sounds	a M2 lower.
E♭	*Alto*	sounds	a M6 lower.
B♭	*Tenor*	sounds	a M9 lower.
E♭	*Baritone*	sounds	an octave and a M6 lower.

The saxophone is a standard instrument in marching and symphonic bands, and is the primary reed instrument in jazz.

scala [It., SKAH-lah] Scale.

scale 1. A series of ascending or descending pitches with a fixed intervallic order (usually stepwise). Scales are the melodic basis of all tonal music. See *diatonic, chromatic scale, major scale, minor scale, pentatonic scale, wholetone scale*. 2. Ratio of diameter to length in an organ pipe. Also known as "scaling." 3. Relationship of a string's sounding length to its intended pitch, in stringed keyboard instruments.

scale degrees Names and numerals given to the degrees of the scale, esp. when they are used as the roots of triads.

The names *tonic, supertonic*, etc. are used also as chord names. For instance, a *dominant* is a chord built on the 5th degree of a scale.

tonic supertonic mediant subdominant

I ii iii IV

dominant submediant subtonic (leading tone)

V vi vii°

scaling See *scale - 2*.

scat In jazz singing, the use of nonsense syllables and unusual vocal effects, e.g. "ba-ba-doo-wop, bop". Scat singing is often instrumental in character.

schalkhaft [G., SHAHLK-hahft] Roguish, playful.

Schall [G., shahl] Sound. *Schallplatte* - phonographic record.

Schellen(trommel) [G., SHEL-en(-trommel)] Tambourine.

scherzando [It., skehr-TSAHN-doh], **scherzhaft** [G., SHEHRTS-hahft] Playful, sportive.

scherzo [It., SKEHR-tsoh] 1. The third movement (usually) of sonatas, symphonies, etc., in vigorous 3/4 meter. A scherzo is most apt to be playful and humorous. Like the minuet, it usually possesses a *trio*. 2. Any playful, sportive piece.

schietto [It., SKYET-toh] Sincere, genuine.

Schlag [G., shlahg] Beat. *Schlagzeug(er)* - percussion(ist).

Schlegel [G., SHLAY-gel] Drumstick, mallet.

schleppend [G., SHLEP-pent] Dragging, heavy.

Schluss [G., shloos] End; cadence.

Schlüssel [G., SHLU(E)S-sel] Clef.

Schmerzhaft [G., SHMEHRTS-hahft] Sorrowful, painful.

Schnarre [G., SHNAHR-reh] Rattle, snare.

schnell [G., shnel] Fast, quick. *schneller* - faster.

Schneller [G., SHNEL-ler] Inverted mordent.

Schottische [G., SHOT-tish-eh] A 19th-century round dance. Also called the "German polka."

schwach [G., shvahkh] Soft, weak.

Schwebung [G., SHVEH-boong] Beat.

Schweigen [G., SHVEI-gent] Rest; silence.

Schweller [G., SHVEHL-ler] Swell.

schwer [G., shvehr] Hard, heavy, difficult.

schwermütig [G., SHVEHR-mu(e)-tikh] Sad, melancholy.

schwungvoll [G., SHVOONG-fohl] Animated, spirited.

sciolto [It., SHOHL-toh] Easy, free.

scordatura [It., skohr-dah-TOO-rah] Non-standard tuning of a stringed instrument. A common example of scordatura is to tune the lowest string down a step; e.g., tuning the low E string of the guitar down to D.

score The printed notation of a composition, where the parts are arranged one beneath the other. A conductor reads from a *score*; the players read from *parts*. Also see *orchestra*.

scucito [It., skoo-CHEE-toh] Detached, *non legato*.

se [It., say] If, whether.

sec [F., sehk], **secco** [It., SEHK-koh] Dry, *staccato*.

sechs [G., zehx] Six.

Sechzehntel [G., ZEHKH-tsehn-tel] Sixteenth note. *sechzehntel Pause* – sixteenth-rest. (See *notes*.)

second See *interval*.

seconda [It., seh-KOHN-dah], **seconde** [F., seuh-goh(n)d] Interval of a second.

second inversion See *inversion*.

secondo [It., seh-KOHN-doh] Second. Also see *primo*.

seelenvoll [G., ZAY-len-fohl] Soulful.

segno [It., SAY-nyoh] Sign. ℅ Used to mark the beginning of a passage to be repeated. See *al segno, da capo, dal segno, fin' al segno*.

segue [It., SAY-gway] 1. Same as *attacca*. 2. Continue in the same manner.

seguidilla [Sp., say-gee-DEE-yah] A Spanish dance in fast 3/4 meter.

sehr [G., zehr] Very.

sei [It., say] Six.

seizième de soupir [F., seh-zee-EHM deh soo-PEER] Sixty-fourth rest. See *notes*.

Sekunde [G., zeh-KOON-deh] Interval of a second.

semi- (L.) Half.

semibiscroma [It., sem-ee-bees-KROH-mah] Sixty-fourth note. (See *notes*.)

semibreve [Brit.] [It., sem-ee-BRAY-veh] Whole note. (See *notes*.)

semicroma [It., sem-ee-KROH-mah] Sixteenth note. (See *notes*.)

semiquaver (Brit.) Sixteenth note. (See *notes*.)

semitone Half step.

semplice [It., SEM-plee-chay] Simple, plain.

sempre [It., SEM-pray] Always.

sensible [F., sah(n)-seebl] Sensitive.

sentito [It., sen-TEE-toh] Expressive.

senza [It., SEN-zah] Without.

septet; Septett [G., zep-TET]; **septetto** [It., sep-TET-toh] 1. A musical composition for seven instruments. 2. A group of seven musicians.

septième [F., seh-TYEHM], **Septime** [G., zep-TEE-meh] Interval of a seventh.

septuor [F., sep-tu(e)-UHR] Septet.

septuplet A group of seven notes played in the time of four (or six).

sequence 1. The immediate repetition of a melodic or harmonic progression at a different pitch, usually a step higher or lower. 2. A complete "performance" of a MIDI recording. See *electronic music*.

sequencer A *sequencer* is a sort of MIDI "tape recorder." Instead of tape, MIDI data is used to record and play back instrumental performances. A sequencer can be either a software program within a computer, or a separate hardware device. Also see *electronic music*.

serenade; serenata [It., say-ray-NAH-tah] Evening music, capable of being performed outdoors. The instrumental serenade usually employs a small number of strings and wind instruments. A well-known serenade is *Eine Kleine Nachtmusik* by Mozart.

sereno [It., seh-REH-noh] Serene, calm.

SERIAL MUSIC

Twentieth-century music which is based on principles other than those of traditional (tonal) music. In serial music, each element of music – pitch, duration, articulation, timbre – is subject to structural control.

The earliest kind of serial technique is the *twelve-tone system* (*dodecaphonic* system), invented by Arnold Schoenberg (1874-1951). It uses a *tone row*, which is a fixed series of 12 notes that must include each member of the chromatic scale. During a composition, no member of the row may be repeated in a voice-part until the other eleven members have appeared. All pitches used in a composition are members of the row, or a form (*permutation*) of the row.

There are four basic permutations of the row: the original, *inversion, retrograde,* and *retrograde inversion.* Transpositions of these permutations are also allowed.

The use of the twelve-tone system generally produces *atonality.* (Tonality is avoided.) Schoenberg's 12-tone music, while being atonal, often uses rather traditional rhythms and forms. Beginning with Anton Webern, however, subsequent serial composers structuralized not only pitch, but also duration, articulation, and timbre, according to their own personal systems of organization.

Also see *Klangfarbenmelodie.*

serial transmission See *electronic music.*

serioso [It., seh-ree-OH-soh] Serious, grave.

service 1. A ritual prescribed for public worship. 2. A musical setting of the church offices, esp. the canticles at morning and evening prayer (Church of England).

sesta [It., SES-tah] Interval of a sixth.

sestetto [It., ses-TET-toh] Sextet.

sestina [It., ses-TEE-nah] Sextuplet.

sette [It., SET-tay] Seven.

settima [It., SET-tee-mah] Interval of a seventh.

seventh See *interval.*

SEVENTH CHORD

A chord containing a 3rd, 5th, and 7th above the root. Below are the principal types:

1. **Dominant seventh**. A seventh chord built on the 5th degree of a major scale; that is, a major triad with a minor 7th above the root. Below is a dominant seventh chord and its inversions:

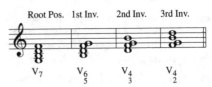

In popular music, dominant seventh chords are represented by the number 7, e.g., D7.

2. **Minor seventh**. A minor triad with a minor 7th above the root.

3. **Half-diminished seventh.** A diminished triad with a minor 7th above the root.

Dm7♭5* or D∅7*

ii°7

4. **Diminished seventh.** A seventh chord built of minor thirds.

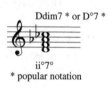

Ddim7 * or D°7 *

ii°7°
* popular notation

Sext(e) [G., zehxt(-eh)] Interval of a sixth.

sextet; Sextett [G., zehx-TET]; **sextuor** [F., sehks-tu(e)-UHR] 1. A musical composition for six instruments. 2. A group of six musicians.

sextuplet; sextolet [F., sehks-tuh-LEH] A group of six notes played in the time of four.

sf, sfz Abbr. for *sforzando.*

sforzando, sforzato [It., sfohr-TSAHN-doh, sfohr-TSAH-toh] Abbr. *sf, sfz* "Forcing" – a sudden strong accent on a note or chord.

sforzando-piano [It., sfohr-TSAHN-doh PYAH-noh] Abbr. *sfp.* A *sforzando* followed immediately by *piano.*

shake Trill.

shanty See *chantey.*

sharp ♯ Raises the pitch of a note by one half step.

sharp, double See *double sharp.*

shawm An ancestor of the oboe, in use until the 17th century.

shift See *position.*

shofar An ancient Jewish instrument made from a ram's horn; it is still in use for ceremonial purposes.

si See *pitch names; solmization.*

siciliana, siciliano [It., see-chee-lee-AH-nah, see-chee-lee-AH-noh] A baroque dance in slow 6/8 or 12/8 meter, similar to the pastorale.

side drum Snare drum.

sight-reading Reading music without having played or practiced it beforehand.

signal Electrical analog of sound.

signature See *key signature; time signature.*

silofono [It., see-LOH-foh-noh] Xylophone.

similar motion See *motion.*

simile [It., SEE-mee-lay] Continue in the same way.

simple meter See *meter.*

sin' al fine [It., seen ahl FEE-nay] Until the end, which is usually indicated by the *segno* (sign).

sine wave Waveform corresponding to a single frequency oscillation. See *electronic music.*

sinfonia [It., seen-foh-NEE-ah] 1. (It.) Symphony. 2. Bach three-part invention. 3. Operatic overture. 4. Introductory movement.

sinfonia concertante [It., seen-foh-NEE-ah kohn-chehr-TAHN-tay] Symphony with one or more solo instruments.

sinfonietta [It., seen-foh-nee-ET-tah] A small symphony.

Singspiel [G., ZEENG-shpeel] Comic opera with spoken dialogue. An example is Mozart's *Die Entführung aus dem Serail* (1782).

sinistra [It., see-NEES-trah] Left (hand).

sino [It., SEE-noh] To; until, as far as.

sitar A lute-like instrument of India, containing melodic as well as drone strings. The sitar is accompanied by *tablas* – small, single-headed drums, played with the hands.

six-four chord Second inversion of a triad. See *inversion*.

sixte [F., seekst] Interval of a sixth.

sixteenth note, rest See *notes*.

sixth See *interval*.

SIXTH CHORD

The first inversion of a triad, e.g., E-G-C.

Neapolitan sixth chord. A major chord, in first inversion, built on the lowered 2nd degree of the scale ($\flat II_6$ chord). It resolves to V.

(or I_6^4):

C: $\flat II_6$ V

Augmented sixth chords. These chords are built on the 6th degree of the scale (in major, the lowered 6th degree) and contain the interval of an augmented sixth, e.g., $A\flat$-$F\sharp$. They also resolve to either V or I_6^4. Following are four basic types:

1. "Italian" 2. "German"

C: IV_{6+} V IV_{6+} V
   (3) $\frac{5}{3}$

3. "French" 4. Doubly-aug. 4th

IV_{6+4+3} V IV_{6+4+3+} I_6^4

With each of the types shown above, the interval of the augmented sixth "expands" to the octave. Although the terms "Italian," "French," and "German" are traditional, they are losing favor among theorists.

sixty-fourth note, rest See *notes*.

skip Melodic progression by an interval larger than a second.

slancio, con [It., kohn SLAHN-syoh] With dash, impetuously.

slargando [It., slahr-GAHN-doh] Slowing down.

slentando [It., slen-TAHN-doh] Slackening, slowing down.

slide 1. Violin playing: The use of *portamento* between two tones – an expressive effect. 2. The movable part of the trombone. Also see *position*.

slur A curved line placed above or below notes to indicate legato.

1. In bowing, a single stroke. (For other meanings, see *bowing*.)

2. Notes taken in a single breath (singing).

3. Phrasing (keyboard music).

When two notes of the same pitch are connected by a curved line, it is called a *tie*. See *tie*.

smorzando [It., smohr-TSAHN-doh] Fading away.

snare drum See *percussion instruments (8)*.

soave [It., soh-AH-vay] Gentle, sweet.

sol See *pitch names*; *solmization*.

sol-fa See *tonic sol-fa.*

solfège [F., suhl-FEHZH], **solfeggio** [It., sohl-FEHJ-joh] The use of vowels or solmization syllables in vocalizing.

solmization Term for systems which use syllables to designate the degrees of the scale. The most common ones are: do, re, mi, fa, sol, la, ti. In the *fixed do* system, *do* is always C (*re* = D, etc.). In the *movable do* system, *do* is always the tonic. For example, in the key of E major, *do* would be *E.*

solo "Alone." 1. A piece for one performer. 2. A solo passage, esp. in orchestral writing.

son (F.) Sound.

sonare [It., soh-NAH-ray] To sound, to ring.

sonata A composition for solo instrument (usually keyboard), or solo instrument and piano, in several movements. The first movement is usually in *sonata form.* The typical sequence of movements is allegro-adagio-minuet or scherzo (optional)-allegro.

SONATA FORM

Sonata form (sometimes called *sonata-allegro* form) is most often used in the first movements of sonatas, symphonies, etc. At the bottom of this page is a diagram of its main sections.

The *exposition* is characterized by a modulation to the dominant (or its equivalent), and it ends with a cadence in that key. The exposition is almost always repeated. The *development* is a modulatory section which serves to increase the drama of the *recapitulation* – which is the decisive return to the tonic key and the restatement of the principal musical ideas presented in the exposition. The recapitulation ends with a cadence on the tonic. Sonata form may be seen, therefore, as A A B A'. (In many classical sonatas, the development and recapitulation together are also repeated; but in practice, this repetition is usually omitted.)

It should be noted that many descriptions of sonata form stress that the exposition must contain a first and second theme. However, many classical sonatas contain only *one* theme in the exposition, or a series of shorter themes, neither of which was considered unusual during the classical period. Therefore, the number of themes in a sonata should not be considered a structural requirement for sonata form.

sonate [F., suh-NAT], **Sonate** [G., zoh-NAH-teh] Sonata.

sonatina, sonatine [F., suh-na-TEEN] A short sonata, usually simple.

song A short, simple, vocal composition which emphasizes the text, as distinct from an *aria,* which is more elaborate.

song cycle A group of related songs which together form a larger work.

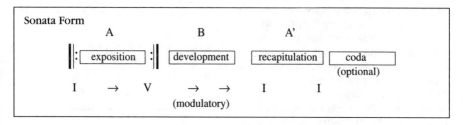

123

song form Ternary form (A B A).

sonore [F., suh-NUHR], **sonoro** [It., soh-NOH-roh] Sonorous, resonant.

sopra [It., SOH-prah] Above. *come sopra* – as above. In piano playing, one hand over the other.

soprano See *voices, range of.* Generally, the highest part or instrument.

soprano clef See *clef.*

soprano saxophone See *saxophone.*

sordamente [It., sohr-dah-MEN-tay] Softly, muted.

sordino [It., sohr-DEE-noh] Mute.

sospirando [It., sohs-pee-RAHN-doh] Sighing, subdued.

sostenuto [It., sohs-tay-NOO-toh] Sustaining the tone; sometimes, slackening the tempo.

sostenuto pedal See *pedal.*

sotto [It., SOHT-toh] Under. *sotto voce* – in an undertone; subdued. In piano playing, one hand under the other.

soul music An American popular music style which developed from black gospel music. Whereas gospel is always religious in nature, soul music usually employs secular lyrics with a more hard-driving beat. Some important contributors to soul music are: Ray Charles, James Brown, and Aretha Franklin.

soundboard In string keyboard instruments (e.g., piano, harpsichord), the wooden board over which the strings are stretched. It acts as a *resonator.*

sound module In electronic music, a sound-producing component designed to produce preset sound types (*programs*). Examples of programs would be "trombone," or "ice rain." Ordinarily each module is assigned its own MIDI channel. A module capable of delivering more than one program at a time is known as a *multi-timbral module*; each

program is assigned its own MIDI channel. Some modules allow the user to edit programs or create new ones. See *electronic music.*

sound post In a viol or violin-family instrument, a small wooden rod set slightly behind the bridge, inside the instrument. It conducts sound from the belly to the back, then reflects it outward through the sound holes.

sound wave The periodic compression and rarefaction of the atmosphere at frequencies discernible to the human ear.

soupir [F., soo-PEER] Quarter rest. See *notes.*

soupirant [F., soo-pee-RAH(N)] Sighing, plaintive.

sourd(e) [F., soor, soord] Muffled, muted.

sourdine [F., soor-DEEN] Mute.

sousaphone A large tuba (helicon) used in marching bands; named after the composer John Philip Sousa, who suggested the design of its bell.

soutenu [F., soo-teuh-NU(E) Sustained.

spacing See *close position.*

spatial notation A notational system in which durations are represented by horizontal distances. For example, a half note may be made equal to one inch of space, a quarter note one-half inch, etc.

In the example below, one inch equals one second of time. A note lasts for the duration of its beam, or until the next note is played.

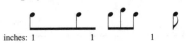

inches: 1　　　　1　　　　1

speech song Same as *Sprechstimme*.

spezzato [It., speh-TSAH-toh] Split, divided.

spianato [It., spyah-NAH-toh] Smooth, even.

spiccato [It., spee-KAH-toh] See *bowing (5)*.

spinet 1. A type of small harpsichord. 2. See *piano, pianoforte*.

spiritoso [It., spee-ree-TOH-soh] Spirited. *con spirito* – with spirit.

spiritual A religious folk song of African-American origin.

Spitze [G., SHPIT-tseh] "Point." Tip of the violin bow.

Spitzflöte [G., SHPITS-flo(e)-teh] "Pointed flute" – a soft organ stop, the pipes of which are conical and pointed at the top.

Sprechstimme, Sprechgesang [G., SHPREHK-shtim-meh, SHPREHK-geh-zang] A vocal style halfway between singing and speech. Approximate pitches are indicated by x-shaped noteheads.

Springbogen [G., SHPRING-boh-gen] Sautillé. See *bowing (4)*.

square wave Waveform consisting of a fundamental and odd-numbered harmonics. See *electronic music*.

Stabat Mater [L., STAH-baht MAH-ter] A liturgical text of the Roman Catholic Church, based on the Crucifixion.

stabile [It., STAH-bee-lay] Firm, steady.

staccato [It., stah-KAH-toh] Detached, separated. Indicated by a dot placed above or below the note.

Also see *bowing*.

staff, stave Pl. staffs, staves. The five horizontal lines used in modern music notation.

Stahlspiel [G., SHTAHL-shpeel] Military glockenspiel.

Ständchen [G., SHTA(E)NT-khen] Serenade.

stanza A division of a poem, in which the lines are grouped together.

stark [G., shtahrk] Strong.

steel band, steel drums A Caribbean band uses *steel drums*, which are specially indented oil drums. By striking the indented areas, a player produces different pitches.

Steg [G., shtehk] Bridge of the violin.

stem See *notes*.

stendendo [It., sten-DEN-doh] Slowing down.

stentando [It., sten-TAHN-doh] With difficulty; heavy, and retarding.

step Progression of a second. See *half step*; *whole step*.

steso [It., STAY-soh] Stretched, spread out, slow.

stesso [It., STEHS-soh] Same.

Stil [G., shteel], **stile** [It., STEE-lay] Style.

Stimme(n) [G., SHTIM-meh(n)] Voice(s).

Stimmung [G., SHTIM-moong] 1. Mood. 2. Tuning.

stop 1. *v.* To press the finger on the string. 2. In organs, *stop* has two meanings: a) the device used to turn on or off a rank of organ pipes; b) a rank of pipes controlled by a *stop*.

stopped pipe A pipe closed at one end. Applies to flue pipes, such as stopped flute and stopped diapason. Also see *organ pipes*.

strain Song, melody, theme.

strascinando [It., strah-shee-NAHN-doh] Dragging.

strathspey A slow Scottish dance in 4/4 meter; a slower type of *reel*.

Streich- [G., shtreikh] Bow; bowed.

strepitoso [It., stray-pee-TOH-soh] Noisy, boisterous.

stretta [It., STRET-tah] A concluding section, taken at a faster tempo.

stretto [It., STRET-toh] See *fugue*.

Strich [G., shtrikh] Bow stroke.

string bass Double bass. See *violin family (4)*.

stringed instruments See *instruments II*.

stringendo [It., streen-JEN-doh] Accelerating.

string quartet 1. Chamber music group consisting of first and second violin, viola, and cello. 2. Composition written for a string quartet.

string quintet 1. Chamber music group consisting of two violins, two violas, and cello. 2. Composition written for a string quintet.

string trio See *trio (2)*.

stromento [It., stroh-MEN-toh] Instrument. pl. *stromenti*.

strophic A song form which has the same music for each stanza of text. Contrasts with *through-composed* from, which has different music for each stanza.

Stück [G., shtu(e)k] Piece, composition.

Stufe [G., SHTOO-feh] Scale degree, step.

Sturm [G., shtoorm] Storm. *stürmisch* – stormy.

style 1. A manner of expression which is characteristic of a historical period, a nation, or a single composer (e.g., baroque *style*). 2. A method of treating one or more of the elements of music (e.g., polyphonic *style*, keyboard *style*).

style galant [F., steel ga-LAH(N)] See *galant style*.

su [It., soo] Above, upon.

sub- [L.] Under, below.

subdominant, subdominant triad 1. The 4th degree of a scale. (See *scale degrees*.) 2. The triad based on the 4th degree of a scale, represented by the numeral IV. The most common combination involving the subdominant is IV-V-I.

subito [It., SOO-bee-toh] Suddenly, quickly.

subject See *fugue*.

submediant See *scale degrees*.

subtonic See *scale degrees*.

suite 1. A baroque instrumental form, consisting of several dance movements. The standard movements of the suite are: *allemande, courante, sarabande,* and *gigue*. The *minuet* is an optional movement, placed usually just before the gigue. Instead of (or in addition to) to the minuet, one or more of the following movements may be used: air, anglaise, *bourrée, gavotte, loure, passepied, polonaise*. 2. Generic term for a multi-movement instrumental composition.

suivez [F., swee-VAY] Follow.

sul, sulla [It., sool, SOOL-lah] On, at, by.

sul ponticello See *bowing (special effects – 1)*.

sul tasto, sulla tastiera See *bowing (special effects – 2)*.

supertonic See *scale degrees*.

sur [It., soor] [F., su(e)r] On, upon, over.

sur la touche See *bowing (special effects –2)*.

suspension See *nonharmonic tones II*.

süss [G., zu(e)s] Sweet.

sussurando [It., soos-soor-AHN-doh] Whispering.

sustain (level) See *envelope; electronic music.*

sustain pedal See *electronic music (keyboard controller).*

sustaining bass pedal Same as *sostenuto pedal.* See *pedal.*

svelto [It., SVEHL-toh] Whispering.

swell organ, swell box, swell pedal Many pipe organs contain a section of pipes enclosed in a large box ("swell box"), which can be opened or closed gradually by a "swell pedal" to effect crescendos and decrescendos. A large pipe organ may have several such mechanisms. The (upper) manual which controls the swell section is called the "swell organ."

swing 1. *v.* In jazz, delaying the second half of the beat, a long-short pattern approximating a triplet feel:

written ♫ ♫   played ♩♪ ♩♪

Generally, the faster the tempo the more even the eighth notes become.

2. The big band jazz style at its peak during the 1930's; intended for dancing. Also see *jazz.*

syllabic See *melisma.*

sympathetic vibration See *resonance.*

symphonic poem A one-movement orchestral composition in a programmatic style, favored by Liszt, R. Strauss, and others.

SYMPHONY
A "sonata" for orchestra. The classical symphony has the following four movements:

*INTRODUCTION (slow)

1. ALLEGRO (sonata form)

2. ADAGIO (ABA)

3. MINUET** w/TRIO
   (optional movement)

4. FINALE (sonata or rondo form)

 * Optional.

** Beethoven's symphonies contain a scherzo instead of a minuet.

Also see *sonata form, minuet, scherzo, rondo.*

syncopation An accent on a weak beat, or between beats. A syncopation is often held over (tied) to a strong beat.

synthesizer A system of electronic instruments which are designed to produce and control sound, usually housed in a single module containing a keyboard, oscillators, computer chips, etc. See *electronic music.*

tabla(s) In Indian music, small single-headed drum(s), played with the hands. Also see *sitar*.

tablature 1. For lutes and guitars, a notational system which uses finger notation rather than pitch notation. In modern guitar tablature, a 6-line staff is used to represent the six strings of the guitar. Numbers are used to indicate the frets:

(Normal notation)

(Tablature)

| 2nd string, 3rd fret | A Major chord | Melodic passage in eighths |

2. Older notational system for keyboard music, using letters or numbers, sometimes combined with notes.

tabor [TAY-ber]A medieval snare drum played with the right hand, while the left hand plays a three-holed pipe; used for dancing.

tace(t) [L.,TAS-it] Be silent.

Takt [G., tahkt] Beat; measure; meter.

tambour [F., tah(n)-BOOR], **tamburo** [It.,tahm-BOO-roh] Drum. *tambour militaire* - snare drum. *tamburo rullante* - tenor drum.

tambourin [F., tah(n)-boor-AH(N)] 1. *Tabor*. 2. An 18th-century French piece imitating the sound of the pipe and tabor. See *tabor*.

tambourine; tambour de basque [F., tah(n)-BOOR deuh bask]; **tamburino, tamburo basco, tamburello** [It., tahm-boo-REE-noh, tahm-BOO-roh BAHS-koh, tahm-boo-REHL-loh]; **Tamburin** [G., tam-boo-REEN] See *percussion instruments (11)*.

tamburo See *tambour*.

tam-tam [It., F., tam tam]; **Tam-tam** [G., tam tam] Gong. See *percussion instruments (14)*.

tangent See *clavichord*.

tango Dance from Argentina in syncopated 2/4 meter.

tanto [It., TAHN-toh] So much, too much.

Tanz [G., tahnts] Dance.

tarantella [It., tah-rahn-TEL-lah] A dance in fast 6/8 meter, from southern Italy.

tardando [It., tahr-DAHN-doh] Slowing.

tardo, tardamente [It., TAHR-doh, tahr-dah-MEN-tay] Slow, slowly.

Taste [G.,TAHS-teh] A key of a keyboard instrument.

tastiera [It., tahs-tee-AY-rah] 1. Fingerboard. 2. Keyboard.

tasto [It., TAHS-toh] 1. A key of a keyboard instrument. 2. The violin fingerboard. For *sul tasto*, see *bowing (special effects - 2)*.

tasto solo [It., TAHS-toh SOH-lo] In *thoroughbass*, unaccompanied bass note(s). Abbr. *t.s.*

technique The mechanical skill of playing or singing.

tedesca [It., teh-DEH-skah] 1. Allemande. Literally, "German." 2. Ländler. *alla tedesca* – in the German style.

Te Deum [L., teh DAY-oom] A song of praise in the liturgy of the Roman Catholic Church.

tema [It., TEH-mah] Theme, subject.

temperament See *equal temperament*.

tempestoso [It., tem-pes-TOH-soh] Tempestuous, stormy.

temple blocks See *Chinese temple blocks*.

tempo [It., TEM-poh] The speed of a composition. Also see *Tempo Indications* at the beginning of this dictionary.

tempo giusto [It., TEM-poh JOOS-toh] In strict time.

tempo primo [It., TEM-poh PREE-moh] Return to the original tempo.

tempo marks See *Tempo Indications* at the beginning of this dictionary.

temps [F., tah(n)] Beat.

teneramente [It., teh-neh-rah-MEN-tay] Tenderly.

tenerezza [It., teh-neh-RET-tsah] Tenderness.

tenor See *voices, range of.*

tenor clef See *clef.*

tenor drum See *percussion instruments (9).*

tenor saxophone See *saxophone.*

tenor trombone See *brass instruments (3).*

tenth See *interval.*

tenuto [It., teh-NOO-toh] Held, sustained. The tenuto mark is an articulation used to show emphasis given to a note or chord :

ternary form See *binary form.*

tertian harmony See *quartal harmony.*

Terz [G., tehrts], **terza** [It., TEHR-tsah] Interval of a third.

Terzett [G., tehr-TSET], **terzetto** [It., tehr-SET-toh] Vocal work for three voices.

terzina [It., tehr-SEE-nah] Triplet.

tessitura [It., tehs-see-TOO-rah] The average range of a vocal part.

tetrachord A series of four scale tones, contained in the interval of a perfect 4th:

C D E F G A B C

The major scale consists of two tetrachords, both of which contain two whole steps followed by a half step.

theme The principal melody in a composition. In fugues the theme is called the *subject*. A theme may also be the basis for a set of variations. (See *variation form.*)

theme and variations See *variation form.*

theory The analysis of music, such as the study of *harmony, counterpoint, form, orchestration.*

theremin An early electronic music instrument (1924), which produced glissando effects.

thesis [Gr., THAY-sis] Downbeat.

third See *interval.*

thirty-second note, thirty-second rest See *notes.*

thoroughbass, figured bass, basso continuo [It., bahs-soh kohn-TEE-noo-oh]

Thoroughbass is the old spelling of "through bass," in the sense of continuing through a piece, as indicated by the Italian term *basso continuo*.

Thoroughbass is a method of indicating the parts that support the melody by means of a bass line and the figures (numbers) below it.

These figures indicate intervals over the bass, and the intended pitches must correspond with the key signature. (For instance, in the key of C, a "6" below the bass note "D" indicates a "B".) Octaves, thirds, and fifths are often omitted in the numbers, since it is assumed that they will be added by the performer. Chromatic alterations: Raised intervals are indicated by a slash through the number or by an accidental; other alterations are indicated by accidentals. Sustained notes are indicated by a horizontal line.

Possible correct realization for the above example:

The thoroughbass system was used extensively during the baroque period, and it is still used today in performing baroque music and (in a modified form) in the study of harmony, where it is usually called *figured bass*. Other names for thoroughbass are *basso continuo*, *fig-ured bass*. During the baroque, thoroughbass was a highly developed art which required improvisation by the performer. A *basso continuo* accompaniment typically employed a harmony instrument (*harpsichord*, small organ, *lute*) and a melodic bass instrument (cello, *viola da gamba*).

through-composed See *strophic*.

thunder machine A percussion instrument used to imitate thunder, consisting of a rotating drum with hard balls inside.

ti See *solmization*.

tie A curved line which connects two successive notes of the same pitch; used to increase the duration of the first note to that of both notes combined.

Also see *slur*.

tief [G., teef] Deep, profound.

tierce [F., tyehrs] Interval of a third.

timbales [tim-BAH-les] 1. Drums similar to bongos, but larger. Played with small sticks. 2. (F.) Timpani.

timbre Tone color. When two different instruments play the same pitch, timbre is the element that makes it possible to distinguish them.

time Loosely used for *meter, duration, tempo*.

time signature Two numbers placed at the beginning of a piece to indicate its meter. The lower number indicates the unit of beat (4 for quarter note, 2 for half note, etc.); the upper number indicates the number of units (beats) in a measure.

timoroso [It., tee-moh-ROH-soh] Timidly.

timpani See *percussion instruments (1)*.

tirare [It., tee-RAH-ray] To draw, as an organ stop, or to slow down.

tirer (v.), **tirez, tiré** [F., tee-RAY] 1. Downstroke of the bow. 2. Same as *tirare*.

toccata [It., tohk-KAH-tah]; **Tokkate** [G., toh-KAH-teh] A keyboard composition in a flowing, improvisational style, often virtuosic.

toccatina [It., tohk-kah-TEE-nah] A short toccata.

tom-toms See *drum set*.

tod, Tod(es-, ten-) [G., toht] Dead, death.

ton [F., toh(n)] Pitch; key; whole tone.

Ton [G., tohn] Tone, pitch, key.

tonal Of or relating to tone, tonality.

tonal answer See *fugue*.

tonality Music which is based on a central triad or tone (tonic). A sense of progression toward or away from the tonic is the fundamental characteristic of tonality. Such music employs the use of keys and is said to be "tonal." Also see *bitonality, polytonality*.

Tonart [G., TOHN-ahrt] Key.

Tondichtung [G., TOHN-dikh-toong] Tone poem.

tone 1. A sound having a definite pitch. 2. The interval of a second: *whole tone* – whole step (major second); *semitone* – half step (minor second). 3. The quality of a musical sound.

tone cluster A group of adjacent tones, played as a single dissonant chord. Tone clusters have been used extensively by 20th-century composers, especially Polish composers such as Lutoslawski and Penderecki.

tone color Same as *timbre*.

tone poem See *symphonic poem*.

tone row See *serial music*.

tonguing With wind instruments, the use of the tongue for articulation. Single tonguing is used at slower tempos; double tonguing (tktk) and triple tonguing (tkt tkt), for faster tempos. The latter two are used mostly by brass players and flutists.

tonic, tonic triad 1. The first degree of a scale (see *scale degrees*); the first and main note of a key (keynote). 2. Triad built on the first degree of a scale, represented by the numeral I.

tonic sol-fa A type of *movable do* solmization system. Also see *solmization*.

Tonika [G., TOH-nee-kah] Tonic.

Tonkunst [G., TOHN-koonst] Music, musical art.

Tonleiter [G., TOHN-lei-ter] Scale.

tono [It., TOH-noh] Tone; whole tone; key; mode.

Tonsatz [G., TOHN-zahts] Composition.

tosto [It., TOH-stoh] Quickly, at once.

touch In keyboard music, the manner in which keys are depressed, e.g., "light," "heavy," "expressive."

touche [F., toosh] One of the keys of a keyboard instrument.

tpt. Abbr. for trumpet.

tr. Abbr. for trill, treble.

track 1. A separate band of tape on which music is recorded. Tape recorders are often referred to by the number of available tracks (4-track, 8-track, etc.). *Multi-track* recording: In recording studios, music is recorded onto separate tracks of tape, which can then be played back together to create the illusion of an ensemble performance. 2. In music sequencers (see *electronic music*), music is recorded electronically onto virtual tracks using MIDI code instead of actual tape.

tracker action In pipe organs, the mechanical action which connects a key to the pipe valve. Electrical actions are also used now.

tranquillo [It., trahn-KWEEL-loh] Tranquil, calm.

transcribe 1. To notate a (recorded) performance as exactly as possible. 2. To convert a composition from one system of notation to another.

transcription 1. Literal arrangement, one that is free of creative additions. 2. An arrangement for a different medium; the conversion of a composition from one system of notation to another.

transition 1. *Bridge passage.* 2. A passing or temporary modulation.

transposing instruments Instruments whose sounding pitch is higher or lower than their written pitch. For transposition pitches of common instruments, see *brass instruments, saxophone, woodwind instruments.*

transposition Playing or rewriting in a key other than the original.

transverse flute Another term for the modern flute.

trascinando [It., trah-shee-NAHN-doh] Dragging, slowing.

trattenuto [It., trah-tay-NOO-toh] Delayed, slowed down.

Trauermusik [G., TRAU-ehr-moo-zeek] Funeral music.

Traum [G., traum] Dream. *träumerisch* – dreamy.

traurig [G., TRAU-rikh] Sad, mournful.

tre [It., tray] Three.

tre corde [It., tray KOHR-day] "Three strings." Cancels the use of the una corda pedal. (See *pedal.*)

treble The highest part; soprano.

treble clef See *clef.*

tremando, tremolando [It., tray-MAHN-doh, tray-moh-LAHN-doh] With a tremolo effect.

tremolo A quick repetition of the same tone. 1. For violins, see *bowing (10).* Also see *ondeggiando.* 2. Keyboard tremolo is produced by a rapid alternation between a tone and its octave (or third, fifth, etc.).

tremulant An organ stop which produces a tremolo effect.

trepak [Russ., treh-PAHK] A Russian dance in fast duple meter.

très [F., treh] Very, much.

triad A three-note chord with a root, a 3rd, and a 5th. Below are the four basic types:

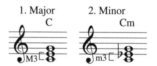

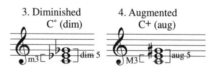

triangle [E.] [F., tree-YAH(n)GL], **Triangel** [G., TREE-ahng-el], **triangolo** [It., tree-AHN-goh-loh] See *percussion instruments (12).*

triangle wave Waveform consisting of a fundamental and odd-numbered harmonics. See *electronic music.*

trill; Triller [G., TRIL-ler]; **trillo** [It., TREEL-loh] An ornament: the rapid alternation of a written note with the second above it.

Abbr. *tr* ⌇⌇ or in baroque music ⌇⌇ Also see *Nachschlag.*

trio 1. A composition in three parts. 2. A group of three musicians. *piano trio* – piano, violin, and cello; *string trio* – violin, viola, and cello. (Haydn's string trios are for two violins and cello). 3. The middle section of a *minuet* or *scherzo*: minuet-trio-minuet repeated.

Triole [G., tree-OH-leh], **triolet** [F., tree-yuh-LEH] Triplet.

trionfale [It., tree-ohn-FAH-lay] Triumphal.

trio sonata Baroque chamber work for three parts, e.g., violin-violin-*thorough-bass* (harpsichord and cello, or harpsichord and viola da gamba, etc.).

triple concerto A concerto for three solo instruments.

triple counterpoint See *invertible counterpoint*.

triple-croche [F., treepl-KRUHSH] Thirty-second note. (See *notes*.)

triple meter See *meter*.

triplet A group of three notes played in the time of two.

tristezza [It., trees-TET-tsah] Sadness, melancholy.

tritone The interval of the augmented fourth (or diminished fifth). Called a *tritone* because it spans three whole-tones. Also see *interval*.

trois [F., trwah] Three.

tromba [It., TROHM-bah] Trumpet, bugle.

trombone See *brass instruments (3)*.

trombone basse [F., troh(n)-BUHN bahs], **trombone basso** [It., trohm-BOH-nay BAHS-soh] Bass trombone.

Trommel [G., TROM-mel] Drum.

Trompete [G., trom-PAY-teh], **trompette** [F., troh(n)-PEHT] Trumpet.

troppo [It., TROHP-poh] Too much. *non troppo* – not too much; *ma non troppo* – but not too much.

troubadour(s) Poet-musicians of southern France (Provence), who were important during the Middle Ages. The music and poetry of the troubadours was devoted to chivalrous love.

trouvère(s) [F., troo-VEHR] Poet-musicians of northern France, who were similar to the troubadours, during the Middle Ages.

trumpet; Trompete [G., trom-PAY-teh], **trompette** [F., troh(n)-PEHT] See *brass instruments (2)*.

tuba See *brass instruments (5)*.

tune Melody.

tuning Adjusting a musical instrument to its proper pitch. When an instrument is properly adjusted, it is said to be "in tune."

tuning fork A two-pronged fork usually pitched at A 440; it produces a pure tone when struck.

turca, alla [It., AHL-lah TOOR-kah] In the Turkish style (military style).

turn An ornament consisting of four (or five) notes which "turn" around a principal note. Here are several versions of the turn and how they are played:

tutti [It., TOOT-tee] All. The full orchestra, as opposed to the soloist.

twelfth An interval: the distance of an octave plus a fifth.

twelve-tone music See *serial music*.

twentieth century music See *History of Western Music*.

tympani Incorrect spelling of *timpani*.

U

über [G., U(E)-behr] Over, above.

Übung [G., U(E)-boong] Study, exercise.

uguale [It., oo-GWAH-lay] Equal, like.

ukulele {yoo-kuh-LAY-lee]A small Hawaiian guitar with four strings.

Umfang [G., OOM-fahng] Compass, range.

umstimmen [G., OOM-shtim-men] Change the tuning.

una corda pedal See *pedal*.

un, una, uno [It., oon, OO-nah, OO-noh] A, one.

un, une [F., eu(n)] A, one.

und [G., oont] And.

undici [It., OON-di-chee] Eleven.

unequal voices Mixed male and female voices.

unison 1. See *interval*. 2. Melody performed at the same pitch by different instruments and/or voices (*all' unisono*).

unisson [F., u(e)-nee-SOH(N)] Unison.

unmerklich [G., OON-mehrk-likh] Imperceptible.

un peu [F., eu(n) PEUH]; **un poco** [It., oon POH-koh] A little.

unruhig [G., OON-roo-ikh] Restless.

unter [G., OON-ter] Below, under.

upbeat One or more notes occurring before the first barline of a piece. Same as *pick-up*.

up-bow See *bowing (1)*. Occasionally spelled *upbow*.

ut [F., u(e)t] See *pitch names*.

ut supra [L., oot SOO-prah] As above, as before.

V

V. Abbr. for vide, violin, voce, voice, volti.

vaghezza, con [It., kohn vah-GET-tsah] With grace, charm.

vago [It., VAH-goh] Vague, lovely.

valse [F., vals] Waltz.

valve On brass instruments, valves are mechanisms which make all chromatic pitches possible by directing the air flow into tubes of various lengths. There are two types of valves: 1) *piston* (trumpet, tuba), 2) rotary (French horn). Most brass instruments have three valves.

vamp An improvised chordal accompaniment, often 2-4 measures repeated ad lib.

variation form A musical form in which a simple melody or *theme* is followed by a set of varied restatements or *variations*. A variation may alter one or more of the following: 1) *Melody* - ornamentation of the theme, use of a new melody, motivic treatment; 2) *Harmony* - a change in the harmonic progression, a modal change (for example, from major to minor); 3) *Tempo* - slow instead of fast; 4) *Character* - a march, dance, etc., variation.

varsovienne [F., var-soh-VYEHN] A slow *mazurka*, named after the city of Warsaw.

vaudeville 1. Satirical song of the 18th century *opéra comique*. 2. Comic variety show.

velato [It., vay-LAH-toh] Veiled, subdued.

veloce [It., vay-LOH-chay] Fast, swift.

vent [F., vah(n)] Wind.

Ventil [G., ven-TEEL] Valve.

Veränderung(en) [G., fehr-A(E)N-dehroong(-en)] Variation(s).

verdoppeln [G., fehr-DOP-peln] To double.

verhallend [G., fehr-HAHL-lent] Fading away.

verismo [It., veh-REEZ-moh] See *opera*.

Verschiebung [G., fehr-SHEE-boong] Una corda pedal.

verschwindend [G., fehr-SHVIN-dent] Disappearing, fading away.

verse; verso [It., VEHR-soh] *Stanza* of a poem. Set to music, each verse uses different words, while the refrain uses the same words.

verse 1
verse 2   refrain
verse 3   (chorus)

verstärken [G., fehr-SHTA(E)R-ken] To reinforce, strengthen.

Vespers The seventh of the canonical hours, sung at sunset. Also see *Office, Divine*.

vezzoso [It., veht-TSOH-zoh] Graceful, elegant.

via [It., VEE-ah] Way, away. *via sordini* - remove mutes.

vibes Short for vibraphone.

vibraphone, vibraharp See *percussion instruments (5)*.

vibration 1. The rapid alternating movement of a body, which produces sound. 2. A single such movement.

The acoustic term for vibration is *oscillation*, esp. when applied to electronic musical instruments.

vibrato A slight fluctuation of pitch or, sometimes, intensity. On violins, it is produced by moving the left hand back and forth while a string is depressed. Vocal vibrato is a slight wavering of tone; the pitch does not change noticeably.

vide [F., veed] Empty, open. *corde à vide* – open string.

viel [G., feel] Much, many.

vier [G., feer] Four.

Viertel [G., FEER-tel] Quarter note. *viertel Pause* – quarter rest. See *notes*.

Vierundsechzigstel (Pause) [G., feer-oon-ZEHKH-tsik-stel] Sixty-fourth note (rest). See *notes*.

vif [F., veef] Lively.

vigoroso [It., vee-goh-ROH-soh] Vigorous, energetic.

villanella [It., veel-lah-NEL-lah]; **villanelle** [F., vee-la-NEHL] A 16th-century vocal work related to folk music, simpler than the *madrigal*.

villanesca [It., veel-lah-NEH-skah] An earlier name for the *villanella*.

vina [VEE-nah] An important instrument of India; a type of lute with four melodic strings and three drone strings.

viol; viole [F., vyuhl] A family of stringed instruments which preceded the violin family (esp. important in the16th-17th c.). Among other differences from the violin family, viols have six strings instead of four and are fretted. The three principal sizes are treble viol, tenor viol, and bass viol (viola da gamba).

viola [E., It., vee-OH-lah] See *violin family (2)*.

viola da gamba [It., vee-OH-lah dah GAHM-bah] See *viol*.

viola d'amore [It., vee-OH-lah dah-MOH-ray] An instrument the size of a treble viol, but with sympathetic strings; held like a violin.

violentemente [It., vee-oh-len-tay-MEN-tay] Violently.

violin; violino [It., vee-oh-LEE-noh], **Violine** [G., vee-oh-LEE-neh] See *violin family (1)*.

VIOLIN FAMILY

The violin family consists of bowed stringed instruments of various sizes. Below are the common orchestral instruments of the violin family, and their ranges.

1. **Violin.** The smallest stringed orchestral instrument and the principal melodic instrument. In orchestral writing, violins are grouped into two sections – 1st and 2nd violins. The violin has four strings, tuned as follows:

sounds as written

2. **Viola.** The alto violin, a little larger than the violin. Its four strings are tuned as follows:

sounds as written

In the orchestra, the viola often provides harmonic support or doubles melodies at the lower octave. The viola is written in alto clef except for high passages, for which the treble clef may be used.

3. **Cello** (violoncello). The bass violin. The cello is too large to be held; it rests on the floor in a more-or-less vertical position. The bass clef is normally used, but tenor clef is not uncommon. Its four open strings are:

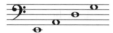

sounds as written

4. **Double bass** (contrabass). The largest member of the violin family. Its four open strings are:

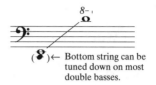

Bottom string can be tuned down on most double basses.

sounds one octave lower

violon [F., vyuh-LOH(N)] Violin.

violoncello [It., vee-oh-lohn-CHEL-loh], **Violoncell** [G., vee-oh-lohn-CHEL], **violoncelle** [F., vyuh-loh(n)-SEHL] Cello.

violone [It., vee-oh-LOH-neh] Large (bass) viola da gamba.

virginal A type of small harpsichord; in late 16th c. England, any harpsichord. Generally applies to instruments whose strings are at right angles to the keys.

virtuoso A performer with extraordinary technique.

vite, vitement [F., veet, veet-MAH(N)] Fast, quickly.

vivace [It., vee-VAH-chay] Quick, lively.

1. Violin   2. Viola   3. Cello   4. Double bass

vivacissimo [It., vee-vah-CHEES-see-moh] Very quick.

vivement [F., veev-MAH(N)] Lively.

vivo [It., VEE-voh] Brisk, lively.

vocalise [F., voh-ka-LEEZ], **vocalization** 1. A technical exercise for the voice, usually sung on vowels only.

vocalize To exercise the voice by singing on vowels only.

voce [It., VOH-chay] Pl. *voci*. Voice. Also see *colla*.

voices, range of The approximate ranges of the human voice are listed above.

These ranges are very often extended in actual practice.

voice-leading The proper progression of voice-parts in a contrapuntal texture.

voicing Pianos: The timbral adjustment of the hammer felts.

Organs: The process of physically manipulating the various parts of the pipe to produce the desired tone quality and intensity.

voilé [F., vwah-LAY] Same as *velato*.

voix [F., vwah] Voice. *voix céleste* – celeste stop of the organ.

volante [It., voh-LAHN-tay] Rushing, flying.

volata [It., voh-LAH-tah] A *run*.

Volkslied [G., FOHLKS-leet] Folk song.

voll [G., fohl] Full.

volles Werk [G., FOHL-les vehrk] Full organ.

volonté, à [F., a vuh-loh(n)-TAY] At will.

volta [It., VOHL-tah] Time. *volta prima* – first time.

voltage controlled amplifier Abbr. VCA. An amplifier whose gain (degree of amplification) may be varied according to a *control voltage*. See *electronic music*.

voltage controlled oscillator Abbr. VCO. An oscillator which can be controlled by another voltage source. See *electronic music*.

volteggiando [It., vohl-teh-jee-AHN-doh] Crossing the hands.

volti subito [It., VOHL-tee SOO-bee-toh] Abbr. *v.s.* Turn (the page) quickly.

volume The measure of amplitude, or loudness, of a sound.

voluntary An organ piece in an improvisational style, used in the church service.

von [G., fohn] By, of, from, on.

vuoto [It., voo-OH-toh] Empty, open. *corda vuota* – open string.

vorbereiten [G., FOHR-beh-rei-ten] To prepare in advance.

vorher [G., FOHR-hehr] Before.

Vorschlag [G., FOHR-shlahk] Appoggiatura. See *Nonharmonic Tones II*.

Vorspiel [G., FOHR-shpeel] Prelude, overture.

Vortrag [G., FOHR-trahk] Execution, delivery.

vorwärts [G., FOHR-va(e)rts] Forward, onward.

Vorzeichnung [G., FOHR-tseikh-noong] Signature.

vox [L., voks] Voice.

W

wachsend [G., VAHK-zent] Growing, increasing.

Waldhorn [G., VALT-hohrn] Hunting horn, or French horn.

waltz A dance in moderate triple meter, very popular since 1800. Waltzes written for the piano usually consist of florid melodic passages in the right hand, accompanied by left-hand chords. Notable composers of waltzes are Chopin, J. Strauss, and Brahms.

Wärme [G., VA(E)R-meh] Warmth.

waveform Graphic representation of a sound wave, showing amplitude and time. See *sawtooth wave, sine wave, square wave*.

wehmütig [G., VAY-mu(e)-tikh] Sad, melancholy.

weich [G., veikh] Soft, gentle.

Weihnachten [G., VEI-nahkh-ten] Christmas. *Weihnachtsmusik* – Christmas music.

wenig [G., VAY-nikh] Little (un poco).

white noise An electronic "hissing" sound. White noise contains all audible frequencies, with randomly distributed amplitudes.

whole note, whole rest See *notes*.

whole step, whole tone A major second, an interval spanning two half steps. See *interval*.

whole-tone scale A six-note scale constructed entirely of whole steps. There are only two whole-tone scales: C-D-E-F♯-G♯-A♯, and D♭-E♭-F-G-A-B. The whole-tone scale was used by impressionist composers, and it has its place in the jazz idiom as well.

wieder [G., VEE-der] Again.

wind chest Organs: An airtight wooden box which transmits air from the bellows to the pipes.

wind instruments See *instruments I, woodwind instruments, brass instruments*.

wind machine A device which imitates the sound of wind, used in music by R. Strauss and Ravel.

wolf 1. An unpleasant tone, the result of a beat between the resonating frequency of the body and the frequency of the tone being produced. The wolf tone can be a problem for cellists. 2. In tuning and temperament, an interval that is unpleasantly out of tune, a result of the particular unequal tuning system employed.

wood block A percussion instrument – a hollow wooden block played with a stick. Also called *Chinese block*.

WOODWIND INSTRUMENTS

Below is a description of the common orchestral woodwind instruments, and their ranges.

1. **Piccolo.** A small flute, with a piercing tone.

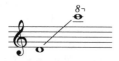

sounds 1 octave higher

2. **Flute.** A cylindrical tube, closed at the upper end. The player blows across an embouchure (side hole). The holes of the flute are stopped by keys. The flute is mellow in its low register and brilliant in its upper register.

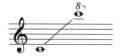

sounds as written

3. **Oboe.** A wooden, conical pipe with a double reed fixed to the upper end. The oboe has a "nasal" tone; it is an effective solo instrument.

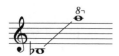

sounds as written

4. **English horn.** An alto oboe, pitched a perfect fifth lower.

sounds a P5 lower

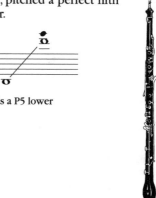

5. **Clarinet.** A cylindrical pipe with a single-reed mouthpiece at one end and a small bell-shaped opening at the other. Its holes are stopped by keys. The clarinet has a fuller tone than the oboe.

B♭ clarinet sounds a M2 lower; *A clarinet* sounds a m3 lower.

6. Bass clarinet. A large clarinet, pitched an octave lower. Its bell is made of metal and curves upward.

when written in treble clef, sounds a M9 lower.

when written in bass clef, sounds a M2 lower.

7. Bassoon. A bass oboewith a large tube that is bent upward. Its dark, full tone is often used to reinforce the cellos; however, it is an extremely agile solo instrument.

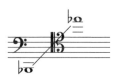

sounds as written

8. Contrabassoon (double bassoon). Pitched an octave below the bassoon. It is a huge instrument, and is only really effective in its powerful low register.

sounds 1 octave lower

wuchtig [G., VOOKH-tikh] Weighty, heavy.

würdig [G., VU(E)R-dikh] Stately, dignified.

XYZ

xylophone See *percussion instruments (3)*.

yodel A singing style, characterized by a rapid alternation between falsetto and chest voice.

Zählzeit [G.,TSA(E)L-tseit] Beat.

zart [G., tsahrt] Delicate, soft.

zehn [G., tsayn] Ten.

Zeitmass [G.,TSEIT-mahs] Tempo.

zelo [It., ZEH-loh] Zeal.

ziemlich [G., TSEEM-likh] Rather, somewhat.

Zigeuner [G., tsee-GOY-nehr] Gypsy.

Zimbel(n) [G.,TSIM-bel(n)] Cymbal(s).

Zingarese, alla [It., AHL-lah tseen-gah-RAY-say] Gypsy style.

zither A stringed instrument consisting of a shallow wooden soundboard with five melody strings and a large number of accompaniment strings. Melody strings, which are closest to the player, are plucked by a finger ring (plectrum) worn on the right thumb.

zögernd [G.,TSO(E)-gehrnt] Hesitating.

zu [G., tsooh] To, too.

Zug [G., tsook] Slide.

zunehmend [G., TSOO-nay-ment] Increasing.

Zunge [G.,TSOONG-eh] Reed.

zurückhalten [G., tsoo-RU(E)K-hahl-ten] To hold back, *rallentando*.

zusammen [G., tsoo-ZAH-men] Together.

zwei [G., tsvei] Two.

Zweiunddreissigstel (Pause) [G., tsvei-oon-DREI-zik-stel (PAU-zeh)] Thirty-second note (rest). See *notes*.

Zwischenspiel [G., TSVISH-en-shpeel] Interlude.

zwölf [G., tsvo(e)lf] Twelve.

Adams, John
1947 - U.S.A.

Albéniz, Isaac
1860-1909 Spain

Alberti, Domenico
ca.1710-1740 Italy

Albinoni, Tomaso
1671-1750 Italy

Alwyn, William
1905-1985 England

Antheil, George
1900-1959 U.S.A.

Arcadelt, Jacob
ca.1505-1568 Netherlands

Arensky, Anton
1861-1906 Russia

Arnold, Malcolm
1921- England

Babbitt, Milton
1916- U.S.A.

Bach, Carl Philipp Emanuel
1714-1788 Germany

Bach, Johann Christian
1735-1782 Germany

Bach, Johann Sebastian
1685-1750 Germany

Bach, Wilhelm Friedemann
1710-1784 Germany

Balakirev, Mily
1837-1910 Russia

Barber, Samuel
1910-1981 U.S.A.

Bartók, Béla
1881-1945 Hungary

Bax, (Sir) Arnold
1883-1953 England

Beach, Amy Marcy Cheney
1867-1944 U.S.A.

Beethoven, Ludwig van
1770-1827 Germany

Bellini, Vincenzo
1801-1835 Italy

Berg, Alban
1885-1935 Austria

Berio, Luciano
1925- Italy

Berkeley, (Sir) Lennox
1903-1989 England

Berlioz, Hector
1803-1869 France

Bernstein, Leonard
1918-1990 U.S.A.

Biber, Heinrich von
1644-1704 Germany-Bohemia

Binchois, Gilles
ca.1400-1460 Burgundy

Bizet, Georges
1838-1875 France

Bliss, (Sir) Arthur
1891-1975 England

Bloch, Ernest
1880-1959 Switzerland; U.S.A.

Blomdahl, Karl-Birger
1916-1968 Sweden

Blow, John
1649-1708 England

Boccherini, Luigi
1743-1805 Italy

Boito, Arrigo
1842-1918 Italy

Bolcom, William
1938- U.S.A.

Borodin, Alexander
1833-1887 Russia

Boulanger, Nadia
1887-1979 France

Bottesini, Giovanni
1821-1889 Italy

Boulez, Pierre
1925- France

Brahms, Johannes
1833-1897 Austria

Britten, Benjamin
1913-1976 England

Brouwer, Leo
1939- Cuba

Brown, Earle
1926- U.S.A.

Bruch, Max
1838-1920 Germany

Bruckner, Anton
1824-1896 Austria

Bull, John
ca.1562-1628 England

Busnois, Antoine
ca.1432-1492 France

Busoni, Ferruccio
1866-1924 Italy

Buxtehude, Dietrich
ca.1637-1707 Germany

Byrd, William
1543-1623 England

Cage, John
1912-1992 U.S.A.

Carissimi, Giacomo
1605-1674 Italy

Carter, Elliott
1908- U.S.A.

Chabrier, Emmanuel
1841-1894 France

Chaminade, Cécile
1857-1944 France

Charpentier, Gustave
1860-1956 France

Charpentier, Marc-Antoine
ca.1636-1704 France

Chausson, Ernest
1855-1899 France

Chávez, Carlos
1899-1978 Mexico

Cherubini, Luigi
1760-1842 Italy

Chopin, Frédéric
1810-1849 Poland; France

Cimarosa, Domenico
1749-1801 Italy

Clementi, Muzio
1752-1832 Italy; England

Copland, Aaron
1900-1990 U.S.A.

Corelli, Arcangelo
1653-1713 Italy

Corigliano, John
1938- U.S.A.

Couperin, François
1668-1733 France

Couperin, Louis
ca.1626-1661 France

Cowell, Henry
1897-1965 U.S.A.

Creston, Paul
1906-1985 U.S.A

Crumb, George
1929- U.S.A.

Crusell, Bernhard Henrik
1775-1838 Finland

Czerny, Carl
1791-1857 Austria

Dallapiccola, Luigi
1904-1975 Italy

Davidovsky, Mario
1934- Argentina; U.S.A.

Davies, (Sir) Peter Maxwell
1934- England

Debussy, Claude
1862-1918 France

De Croes, Henri Jacques
1705-1786 France

de Falla, Manuel
1876-1946 Spain

Delibes, Léo
1836-1891 France

Delius, Frederic
1862-1934 England

Dello Joio, Norman
1913- U.S.A.

Denisov, Edison
1929-1996 Russia

Diabelli, Antonio
1781-1858 Austria

Diamond, David
1915- U.S.A.

d'Indy, Vincent
See Indy, Vincent d'

Dittersdorf, Karl Ditters von
1739-1799 Austria

Dodge, Charles
1942- U.S.A.

Dohnányi, Ernst von
1877-1960 Hungary; U.S.A.

Donizetti, Gaetano
1797-1848 Italy

Dowland, John
1563-1626 England

Druckman, Jacob
1928-1996 U.S.A.

Dufay, Guillaume
ca.1400-1474 Burgundy

Dukas, Paul
1865-1935 France

Dunstable, John
ca.1385-1453 England

Dvořák, Antonín
1841-1904 Czechoslovakia

Elgar, (Sir) Edward
1857-1934 England

Enescu, Georges (Enesco)
1881-1955 Rumania

Fauré, Gabriel
1845-1924 France

Feldman, Morton
1926-1987 U.S.A.

Fibich, Zdeněk
1850-1900 Czechoslovakia

Field, John
1782-1837 Ireland

Fine, Irving
1914-1962 U.S.A.

Finney, Ross Lee
1906- U.S.A.

Finzi, Gerald
1901-1956 England

Floyd, Carlisle
1926- U.S.A.

Foote, Arthur
1853-1937 U.S.A.

Foss, Lukas
1922- U.S.A.

Françaix, Jean
1912- France

Franck, César
1822-1890 Belgium; France

Frescobaldi, Girolamo
1583-1643 Italy

Froberger, Johann Jakob
1616-1667 Austria

Gabrieli, Giovanni
ca.1554-1612 Italy

Gade, Niels Wilhelm
1817-1890 Denmark

German, (Sir) Edward
1862-1936 England

Gershwin, George
1898-1937 U.S.A.

Gesualdo, Don Carlo
ca.1560-1613 Italy

Gibbons, Orlando
1583-1625 England

Gilbert, (Sir) William S.
1836-1911 England &

Sullivan, (Sir) Arthur
1842-1900 England

Ginastera, Alberto
1916-1983 Argentina

Giuliani, Mauro
1781-1829 Italy

Glass, Philip
1937- U.S.A.

Glazunov, Alexander
1865-1936 Russia

Glinka, Mikhail Ivanovich
1804-1857 Russia

Gluck, Christoph Willibald
1714-1787 Germany

Górecki, Henryk-Mikolaj
1933- Poland

Gottschalk, Louis Moreau
1829-1869 U.S.A.

Gould, Morton
1913-1996 U.S.A.

Gounod, Charles
1818-1893 France

Grainger, Percy
1882-1961 Australia; U.S.A.

Granados, Enrique
1867-1916 Spain

Grieg, Edvard
1843-1907 Norway

Griffes, Charles Tomlinson
1884-1920 U.S.A.

Grofé, Ferde
1892-1972 U.S.A.

Guerra, Gerardo Gombau
1906-1971 Spain

Gurlitt, Cornelius
1820-1901 Germany

Handel, George Frideric
1685-1759 Germany; England

Hanson, Howard
1896-1981 U.S.A.

Harbison, John
1938- U.S.A.

Harris, Roy
1898-1979 U.S.A.

Harrison, Lou
1917- U.S.A.

Haydn, Franz Joseph
1732-1809 Austria

Haydn, Michael
1737-1806 Austria

Heller, Stephen
1814-1888 Hungary

Henze, Hans Werner
1926- W. Germany

Hindemith, Paul
1895-1963 Germany; U.S.A.

Holst, Gustav
1874-1934 England

Honegger, Arthur
1892-1955 France

Hovhaness, Alan
1911- U.S.A.

Howells, Herbert
1892-1983 England

Hummel, Johann Nepomuk
1778-1837 Austria

Humperdinck, Engelbert
1854-1921 Germany

Ibert, Jacques
1890-1962 France

Indy, Vincent d'
1851-1931 France

Ireland, John
1879-1962 England

Isaac, Henricus
1450-1517 Netherlands

Ives, Charles
1874-1954 U.S.A.

Janáček, Leoš
1854-1928 Czechoslovakia

Janequin, Clément
ca.1485-1558 France

Jolivet, André
1905-1974 France

Joplin, Scott
1868-1907 U.S.A.

Josquin des Prez
ca.1440-1521 Netherlands

Kabalevsky, Dmitri
1904-1987 Russia

Kagel, Mauricio
1931- Argentina; Germany

Khatchaturian, Aram
1903-1978 Armenia

Kirchner, Leon
1919- U.S.A.

Knussen, Oliver
1952- England

Koechlin, Charles
1867-1950 France

Kodály, Zoltán
1882-1967 Hungary

Köhler, Louis
1820-1886 Germany

Kolb, Barbara
1939- U.S.A.

Korngold, Erich Wolfgang
1897-1957 Austria; U.S.A.

Kraft, William
1923- U.S.A.

Kreisler, Fritz
1875-1962 Austria; France

Krenek, Ernst
1900-1991 Austria; U.S.A.

Krommer, Franz
1759-1831 Moravia

Kubik, Gail
1914-1984 U.S.A.

Kuhlau, Friedrich
1786-1832 Germany; Denmark

Lalo, Édouard
1823-1892 France

Landini, Francesco
1325-1397 Italy

Langgard, Rued
1893-1952 Denmark

Larsson, Lars-Erik
1908-1986 Sweden

La Rue, Pierre de
ca.1460-1518 Netherlands

Lassus, Orlande (Orlando di Lasso)
1532-1594 Netherlands

Leclair, Jean-Marie
1697-1764 France

Lehár, Ferencz (Franz)
1870-1948 Hungary

Leoncavallo, Ruggiero
1857-1919 Italy

Ligeti, György
1923- Hungary

Liszt, Franz
1811-1886 Hungary

Lloyd, George
1913- England

Luening, Otto
1900-1996 U.S.A.

Lully, Jean-Baptiste
1632-1687 France

Lutoslawski, Witold
1913-1994 Poland

MacDowell, Edward
1861-1908 U.S.A.

Machaut, Guillaume de
ca.1300-1377 France

Mahler, Gustav
1860-1911 Austria

Marais, Marin
1656-1728 France

Marcello, Alessandro
1669-1747 Italy

Marenzio, Luca
1553-1599 Italy

Martin, Frank
1890-1974 Switzerland

Martinu, Bohuslav
1890-1959 Czechoslovakia

Martirano, Salvatore
1927- U.S.A.

Mascagni, Pietro
1863-1945 Italy

Massenet, Jules
1842-1912 France

Medtner, Nikolai
1880-1951 Russia

Mendelssohn (-Hensel), Fanny
1805-1847 Germany

Mendelssohn (-Bartholdy), Felix
1809-1847 Germany

Mennin, Peter
1923-1983 U.S.A.

Menotti, Gian-Carlo
1911- Italy

Mercadante, (Giuseppe) Saverio
1795-1870 Italy

Messiaen, Olivier
1908-1992 France

Meyerbeer, Giacomo
1791-1864 Germany

Milhaud, Darius
1892-1974 France

Moeran, E.J. (Ernest John)
1894-1950 England

Monte, Philippe de
1521-1603 Netherlands

Monteverdi, Claudio
1567-1643 Italy

Morley, Thomas
ca.1557-1602 England

Mozart, Leopold
1719-1787 Germany

Mozart, Wolfgang Amadeus
1756-1791 Austria

Mussorgsky, Modest
1839-1881 Russia

Musgrave, Thea
1928- Scotland

Myaskovsky, Nikolay
1881-1950 Russia

Nancarrow, Conlon
1912- Mexico

Nielsen, Carl
1865-1931 Denmark

Nilsson, Bo
1937- Sweden

Nono, Luigi
1924-1990 Italy

Nørgard, Per
1932- Denmark

Obrecht, Jacob
ca.1451-1505 Netherlands

Ockeghem, Johannes
ca.1410-1497 Netherlands

Offenbach, Jacques
1819-1880 France

Oliveros, Pauline
1932- U.S.A.

Orff, Carl
1895-1982 Germany

Pachelbel, Johann
1653-1706 Germany

Paderewski, Ignace Jan
1860-1941 Poland

Paganini, Niccolò
1782-1840 Italy

Palestrina, Giovanni
ca.1525-1594 Italy

Palmgren, Selim
1878-1951 Finland

Parry, (Sir) (Charles) Hubert (Hastings)
1848-1918 England

Pärt, Arvo
1935- Estonia

Partch, Harry
1901-1974 U.S.A.

Penderecki, Krzysztof
1933- Poland

Pergolesi, Giovanni Battista
1710-1736 Italy

Perle, George
1915- U.S.A.

Persichetti, Vincent
1915-1987 U.S.A.

Pfitzner, Hans
1869-1949 Germany

Philippe de Vitry
1291-1361 France

Piazzola, Astor
1921-1992 Argentina

Piccinni, Niccolò
1728-1800 Italy

Piston, Walter
1894-1976 U.S.A.

Ponce, Manuel
1882-1948 Mexico

Ponchielli, Amilcare
1834-1886 Italy

Poulenc, Francis
1899-1963 France

Pousseur, Henri
1929- Belgium

Prez, Josquin des
See Josquin des Prez

Prokofiev, Sergei
1891-1953 U.S.S.R.

Puccini, Giacomo
1858-1924 Italy

Purcell, Henry
1659-1695 England

Quantz, Johann Joachim
1697-1773 Germany

Rachmaninoff, Sergei
1873-1943 Russia

Raff, Joachim
1822-1882 Germany

Rameau, Jean-Philippe
1683-1764 France

Ravel, Maurice
1875-1937 France

Read, Gardner
1913- U.S.A.

Rebikov, Vladimir
1866-1920 Russia

Reger, Max
1873-1916 Germany

Reich, Steve
1936- U.S.A.

Reinecke, Carl
1824-1910 Germany

Respighi, Ottorino
1879-1936 Italy

Reynolds, Roger
1934- U.S.A.

Rheinberger, Josef
1839-1901 Germany

Riegger, Wallingford
1885-1961 U.S.A.

Riley, Terry
1935- U.S.A.

Rimsky-Korsakov, Nikolai
1844-1908 Russia

Rochberg, George
1918- U.S.A.

Rodrigo, Joaquín
1901- Spain

Rore, Cipriano di
1516-1565 Netherlands; Italy

Rorem, Ned
1923- U.S.A.

Rossini, Gioacchino
1792-1868 Italy

Roussel, Albert
1869-1937 France

Rózsa, Miklós
1907- Hungary; U.S.A.

Rubinstein, Anton
1829-1894

Ruggles, Carl
1876-1971 U.S.A.

Saint-Saëns, Camille
1835-1921 France

Salieri, Antonio
1750-1825 Italy; Austria

Sarasate, Pablo de
1844-1908 Spain

Satie, Erik
1866-1925 France

Scarlatti, Alessandro
1660-1725 Italy

Scarlatti, Domenico
1685-1757 Italy; Spain

Schoenberg, Arnold
1874-1951 Austria; U.S.A.

Schnittke, Alfred
1934- Russia

Schoek, Othmar
1886-1957 Switzerland

Schubert, Franz
1797-1828 Austria

Schuller, Gunther
1925- U.S.A.

Schuman, William
1910-1992 U.S.A.

Schumann, Clara (Wieck-)
1819-1896 Germany

Schumann, Robert
1810-1856 Germany

Schütz, Heinrich
1585-1672 Germany

Schwantner, Joseph
1943- U.S.A.

Scriabin, Alexander
1872-1915 Russia

Serocki, Kazimierz
1922-1981 Poland

Sessions, Roger
1896-1985 U.S.A.

Shostakovitch, Dmitri
1906-1975 Russia

Sibelius, Jean
1865-1957 Finland

Smetana, Bedrich
1824-1884 Bohemia

Soler, Padre Antonio
1729-1783 Spain

Sousa, John Philip
1854-1932 U.S.A.

Spohr, Ludwig (Louis)
1784-1859 Germany

Stamitz, Johann
1717-1757 Germany

Stanford, (Sir) Charles Villiers
1852-1924 Ireland

Starer, Robert
1924- Austria; U.S.A.

Stenhammar, Wilhelm
1871-1927 Sweden

Still, William Grant
1895-1978 U.S.A.

Stockhausen, Karlheinz
1928- W. Germany

Strauss (II), Johann
1825-1899 Austria

Strauss, Richard
1864-1949 Germany

Stravinsky, Igor
1882-1971 U.S.S.R.; U.S.A.

Subotnick, Morton
1933- U.S.A.

Suk, Josef
1874-1935 Czechoslovakia

Suppé, Franz von
1819-1895 Austria

Sweelinck, Jan Pieterszoon
1562-1621 Holland

Szymanowski, Karol
1882-1937 Poland

Tailleferre, Germaine
1892-1983 France

Takemitsu, Toru
1930- Japan

Tallis, Thomas
ca.1505-1585 England

Tansman, Alexandre
1897-1986 Poland; France

Tartini, Giuseppe
1692-1770 Italy

Tavener, John
1944- England

Taverner, John
ca.1490-1545 England

Tchaikovsky, Peter Ilyich
1840-1893 Russia

Tcherepnin, Alexander
1899-1977 Russia; U.S.A.

Telemann, Georg Philipp
1681-1767 Germany

Thompson, Virgil
1896-1989 U.S.A.

Tippett, (Sir) Michael
1905- England

Tomasi, Henri
1901-1971 France

Torelli, Giuseppi
1658-1709 Italy

Tower, Joan
1938- U.S.A.

Tubin, Eduard
1905-1982 Estonia

Turina, Joaquín
1882-1949 Spain

Ussachevsky, Vladimir
1911-1990 Russia; U.S.A.

Varèse, Edgard
1883-1965 France; U.S.A.

Vaughn Williams, Ralph
1872-1958 England

Verdi, Giuseppe
1813-1901 Italy

Vierne, Louis
1870-1937 France

Villa-Lobos, Heitor
1887-1959 Brazil

Vivaldi, Antonio
1678-1741 Italy

Wagner, Richard
1813-1883 Germany

Waldteufel, Emil
1837-1915 France

Walton, (Sir) William
1902-1983 England

Weber, Karl Maria von
1786-1826 Germany

Webern, Anton
1883-1945 Austria

Weill, Kurt
1900-1950 Germany

Wen-chung, Chou
1923- U.S.A.

Widor, Charles-Marie
1844-1937 France

Wieniawski, Henryk
1835-1880 Poland

Wilbye, John
1574-1638 England

Willaert, Adrian
ca.1490-1562 Netherlands

Wolf, Hugo
1860-1903 Austria

Wuorinen, Charles
1938- U.S.A.

Xenakis, Iannis
1922- Greece

Yun, Isang
1917-1995 Korea; Germany

Zemlinsky, Alexander (von)
1871-1942 Austria

Zwilich, Ellen Taaffe
1939- U.S.A.